# THE DOWNERS OF SOUTH AUSTRALIA

# The Downers of South Australia

Alick Downer

Wakefield Press
1 The Parade West
Kent Town
South Australia 5067
www.wakefieldpress.com.au

First published 2012



Edited by Laura Andary
Cover design by Alice James
Typeset by Wakefield Press
Printed by Openbook Howden Design & Print, Adelaide

ISBN 978 1 74305 199 3

*To my grandchildren*

Henry Philip Clauson
Arabella Mary Clauson
Betram Alexander Havelock Steens
Georgina Mary Beatrice Downer

# Contents

# Foreword

My father, Sir Alexander Downer, wrote this book in the years before his death in 1981. He often described himself as an amateur historian and his love of history extended to the history of his own family.

For years, Sir Alexander – or Alick as he was known – tried to find the precise origin of the Downer family. The first chapter of the book describes his quest to find the roots of the family. Since his death, I have been able to discover the exact origins of the South Australian Downers.

Henry Downer and his bride Jane Field were married in the parish church in Alverstoke in Hampshire. The church itself was rebuilt between 1863 and 1865. Alverstoke these days is a middle class suburb of what has now become the Portsmouth/Gosport conurbation.

When I visited Alverstoke some years ago I came across the parish priest. I told him my great grandfather had married in the church. He regarded this as a great coincidence. A distinguished South Australian, Sir Henry Ayers, had been married in the same church. That may not, of course, have been the coincidence it appeared to be. The Ayers and Downer families may well have known each other and the Downer's successful transition to Australia may well have played its part in encouraging the Ayers to migrate.

Portsmouth was and still is Britain's great naval base. Sailors would have returned to Portsmouth with reports of Australia and the other corners of the third world. Henry Downer, who was a naval tailor, must have thought things could only get better if he tried out South Australia. It was a brave and risky decision but it worked for him.

Alick Downer was a family man. Not only was he a loving father and husband, but he also swore by the old aphorism 'Man is an omnibus in which all of his ancestors travel.' He believed family personality traits were passed down from one generation to the next. In the case of the Downers, he was something of a chauvinist; he believed that on balance the Downers were a good and able people.

That is certainly true of some of them. But his vision of the family was, perhaps, a little dewy eyed. Faults were varnished into minor peccadilloes and family members of rather average ability were upgraded to able! There's no harm in that; he was immensely proud of his family.

The Downer family has been seen by the community as part of the backbone of conservative South Australia. An intensely political family who saw public service as public duty, they were certainly believers in King or Queen, Empire and country. No Downer is recorded as being a passionate republican. The Downers also saw themselves as British in a broad cultural sense and were proud of that British heritage. And none would have relished the decline of the British Empire.

Beyond those verities, the Downers were nevertheless reformers when they believed reform was needed. And they were not a family driven by intolerance and bigotry. They were, for their times, entirely reasonable people.

Alick Downer's book is an interesting historical study of a family whose views have, of course, evolved as circumstances and values have changed. That must be true of every family. But this book helps to explain how that has happened.

These days, the Downer family is less South Australian and more Australian than ever before. An inevitable consequence of technology and globalisation. In my direct family, only my mother – the author's widow – and I live in South Australia. Two of my sisters live in Sydney and one in America. Two of my children live in Sydney, one in Tokyo and one in London.

That may say something about the Downer family; they are, in the main, people of honest ambition, pragmatic and contributors to building Australia in many different ways.

Alexander Downer, October 2012

# Preface

The purpose of this book is to tell my children, grandchildren, and those who come after them, something of the lives and careers of their antecedents. For the past forty years, I have tried to gather information about my family; a task made more difficult by their lack of records. Most of what they left has been lost, destroyed or burnt. In my youth, elderly relations willingly gave me recollections from childhood, and things told to them by their parents. In England, I have researched periodically within my means, and this I will continue, but genealogy nowadays is an expensive occupation. In Australia, the Archives Department in Adelaide, early newspapers and the National Library in Canberra have proved useful; so has the family tree compiled by my cousin Tom Downer together with his lively interest in our forbears.

A good deal of what follows is autobiographical, being an interpretation of my relations I knew best. A disproportionate amount is about myself, which I regret: had I possessed more material on the pioneer Downers and our English origins, more justice would have been done to these courageous personalities. Perhaps my own political and diplomatic career may interest sections of the public as well as my own descendants; certainly the distinguished life of Sir John Downer is of importance to students of Australian history and politics.

I am indebted to Dr John Playford of the Politics Department, Adelaide University, for his help in recent years, to my daughter Stella Stevens who typed part of the first draft of the manuscript and to Mrs Heather Simpson for her excellent typing and secretarial assistance. If some of my more remote connections feel aggrieved by not being included, I apologise in advance; my intention throughout has been to concentrate principally on those Downers who have engaged in public affairs.

## *Chapter 1*

# Origins

Downer is a name of ancient origin in England, if not of any notable distinction. The earliest references I have seen are in the fourteenth century to Robert le Downer, Ralph le Douner, and Stephen le Downar, the latter in 1327. Researchers into English surnames say it means 'a dweller by the downs'. Sir Phillip Kerr, then Garter King of Arms, told me in 1938 that at first the name would have been 'Down': the suffix 'er' being added later. This is also the view of PA Reaney in his *The Origin of English Surnames.* Apparently, the 'er' along with other appendages, became usual to describe a man's place of residence; it was applied particularly to country names borne by smaller farmers and rural workers in Kent, Sussex and Hampshire.

In Henry VIII's reign, the name is variously mentioned. At Eltham in Kent, John Downer was buried in 1516 near to the high altar. In his will, tapers were to be burnt to various saints; he left his house and croft to his wife Margaret with remainder to his son Robert. He mentions his daughters Elen and Eleanor; a little house adjoining the kitchen is given to the parish clerk of Eltham to dwell in forever. Again, in 1526, another John Downer of Eltham made bequests to his wife Agnes, his son John, and a house and land to his daughter Agnes. Later, in 1544 in a will proved at Rochester, John Downer declared his wife Elizabeth to have tenement and lands in Eltham for ten years; they were then to go to J Petley and his heirs.

A publication in the Bodleian Library entitled *Alumni Oxonienses, members of the University of Oxford 1500–1714*, a matriculation register, mentions Thomas Downer of London, St John's College, taking his BA degree in 1604, followed by his MA in 1608, and then becoming a parson. Howard, son of Edward Downer of Southampton, is recorded as studying as Balliol, later at Wadham, with similar academic success in 1681 and 1684. Another Thomas Downer, of Berwick, Northumberland, matriculated in 1626.

For centuries the name has occurred in the southern countries of England. For example, in the village churchyard of Kirdford. In Sussex, there were several old Downer graves when I first visited it in 1938. Nearby, at Marshall's Farm, the tenant farmer, a Downer, told me that his forbears had rented this farm from the Leconfield Estate since the seventeenth century. There have been families in the neighbourhoods of Arundel, Storrington, Chichester, Southampton, the Isle of Wight, Downton in Wiltshire (a picturesque thatched roof house near the centre of the village bears the name *Downers*), Hertfordshire, and elsewhere. But according to Sir Anthony Wagner, the recent Garter King of Arms, it seems to be essentially a local name concentrated in West Sussex, Hampshire and East Wiltshire.

There was also an emigration of Downers to the United States as early as 1650. At the beginning of the 1900s, a society was formed called 'The Downers of America' with headquarters at Ann Arbor, Michigan. Its objects were 'To unite in closer bonds all Downers and especially the descendants of Robert Downer of Newberrypoot, Massachusetts'. Writing to me in 1955, the Director of the Michigan Historical Museum said that the Downers who came to America arrived in 1650 and originally lived near Salisbury, Wiltshire. He added that there are records of eleven families having settled in Washtenaw County, Michigan. Downersgrove, a town some thirty miles from Chicago, was founded by Robert Downer's descendants.

An echo of this occurred in 1909. Frank H Downer, in a letter from London on 30 December to his uncle Sir John in Adelaide wrote:

> I sometimes meet in the City a Mr Davis … and the other day he told me an amusing coincidence. Davis was staying

> at a hotel on the Continent and he there noticed a clean shaven, strong faced man whose face seemed familiar, and he noticed that this man was continually looking at him. Afterwards, the stranger spoke to him … Davis asked his name and he said it was George William Downer. This chap said he was an American. He knew all the names of the Downers in Adelaide and of their family, and said that he had traced up the families and he had learnt that one family went to Australia, and the other (his) to America. Davis said he was very much like you.

None of my inquiries had been successful in ascertaining whether the 'Downers of America' still exists as an organisation. But it is interesting to note that they display the same coat of arms as used by South Australian Downers and as recorded in *Robson's British Herald of the Armorial Bearings of the Nobility and Gentry of Great Britain and Ireland*, published in 1830. The presumption is that we are descended from the same stem, but the evidence is too sketchy to claim this with certainty.

One of the difficulties in writing about our ancestors is the absence of records. They must have been modest people who went to South Australia in 1838, unaware of their historical importance as pioneers of part of what was destined to become one of the great countries in the world. Whatever they left behind, apart from some fine pieces of furniture, has either been lost or destroyed: I regret to say that until my own time, most members of our family have been lamentably careless in maintaining records of their activities.

Who were our forbears before embarking for the infant colony of South Australia? My father, Sir John, used to say that they were yeoman farmers in the south of England. My cousin, Marion Downer, thought so too, believing they came from Wiltshire, but so far I have not succeeded in tracing where they lived. The earliest member of our family of whom we have any sure knowledge is Mary Ann Downer, mother of Henry Downer. She was born in 1792 and came to Adelaide to look after her son and his children in the early 1860s, following Mrs

Henry Downer's death in 1861. Mary Ann lived in the family house on South Terrace until her own demise on 27 July 1868. Henry, who was born in 1811 when she was only nineteen, was probably her eldest child; her husband's Christian name has vanished. I do not know for certain whether there were other children from her marriage. Marion Downer, when an old lady, told me that there were two other sons who subsequently came to South Australia. One was named Edward, who settled in Port Pirie. If this is so, I have never heard any of my relations refer to them.

My knowledge of Mary Ann is confined to what my mother told me; of how my father complained about always being given one of the last cups of tea from the pot – a fate, no doubt, shared by many a second youngest boy in a large family. I gather he rather resented her taking, in some degree, his mother's place. But whatever her merits and defects, she must have been a woman of courage and devotion to undertake the long, uncomfortable voyage from England in 1862, at the age of seventy, doubtless convinced she would never see home again, resolved to keep house for her bereaved son and those of her grandchildren who were still unmarried, notably two brilliant school boys, John and Harold.

## *Chapter 2*

# Pioneer Ancestors: Henry and Jane Downer

It must have been 1837 when Henry and Jane Downer decided to uproot themselves from all they had been accustomed to in English life, and embark for a little known distant land. The South Australian Foundation Act had been passed by the British Parliament in August 1834. Delays arising out of dissensions between the Colonial Office, the Board of Commissioners established by the Act, and The South Australian Company, resulted in the Colony not being proclaimed until the arrival of the first Governor, Captain John Hindmarsh RN, in HMS *Buffalo* on 28 December 1836. By this time some publicity had been given in England to the activities of the Commissioners in their endeavours to settle the Colony by the then novel idea first suggested by Edward Gibbon Wakefield of selling the land for a nominal sum and using the proceeds to bring out emigrants.

It seems that the Downers were attracted by these ideas. Probably a spirit of adventure more than any other motive, induced them to try their luck in the new world. Not that England in 1837 would have been unpleasant for living. The turbulence caused by the Napoleonic Wars, which had ended some twenty-two years before, had subsided. The long struggle for parliamentary reform had been finally won in 1832. What was to prove a new era of monarchy began in June, when the eighteen-year-old Victoria succeeded her bluff, amiable, but rather bawdy uncle William as a sovereign. The government was led by Lord Melbourne, a statesman who, if inclined to indolence at least showed a wisdom and tact lacking in some of his twentieth century successors.

There are no records to show their permanent home at this period, but there is some evidence to suggest that they were living in Portsmouth where their second son, Henry was born on 22 March 1836. It was from Portsmouth that they sailed in the *Eden* on 24 February 1838.

The *Eden* was a barque of 527 tons under the command of Captain J Cook. From Colonel Light's drawing of her at anchor in Port Adelaide, she showed graceful lines. She carried fare-paying passengers together with emigrants proceeding under the Wakefield scheme. Henry Downer was a man of some substance; he and his family paid their own way. The ship must have been crowded with two hundred and twenty five passengers in all, but amongst them were people who became well-known early settlers as well as family friends: Philip and Edmund Levi, John Moses Phillipson, Joseph Brooks, JS Bagshaw, John Ragless and Charles Beck.

The voyage was made via the Cape, and the size and complement of the ship would have heightened the discomfort. The Downers had two children on board: Charles, their eldest boy born in 1834, and Henry. In those days, passengers were expected to furnish their own cabins for the most part, but even personal possessions could hardly relieve the tedium of living in cramped quarters in the company of so many for so long a time. It was winter when they sailed; it was the southern winter when they landed at Holdfast Bay on 24 June 1838, exactly four months after sailing down Spithead.

Unhappily, we are deprived of letters and diaries which might have recorded their experiences of their final parting from England and of life at sea. Henry and Jane were never to see their home country again. What, in particular, did Jane Downer feel as the *Eden* coasted past the Isle of Wight whence she came? Her maiden name was Field, and she was between four and five years older than her husband, being born in 1806 or 1807. The Fields lived on the Isle of Wight, and had some interesting connections. One was the poet Thomas Chatterton;

another named Field, a cousin, was a member of the House of Commons in the latter part of the nineteenth century. As to her appearance and character, I know little. She must have been a woman of great spirit with a warm nature and deep love for her family. She became the mother of seven children, was a loyal and devoted wife to Henry throughout his various vicissitudes, and was to die prematurely in Adelaide when only fifty-four years old on 4 January 1861. Across the chasm of one hundred years and more, which divided Jane Downer from my generation, I have often felt a strong attraction towards her. Unquestionably she contributed great qualities to her children and all of us who are her descendants. Though neither she nor Henry lived to see it, the future was to show that in their sons, they give Australia attributes of mind, talent and achievement, such as happens only rarely in any country in a single generation.

When the Downers landed at Holdfast Bay, near what Governor Hindmarsh not long before had christened 'Adelaide', the total population of the colony numbered little more than four thousand. The Union Jack had been hoisted only eighteen months previously; houses and buildings were few, amounting to merely three hundred and fifty; most of the incoming settlers perforce had to accommodate themselves in tents. I do not know for certain where Henry and Jane first lived, but it was said to be near Hindmarsh, across the River Torrens. Life must have been more difficult in the months that followed, for during the voyage, Jane had become pregnant in addition to having to care for Charles aged four, and young Henry aged two. What is certain is that by 1839, Henry had established himself in business as a tailor, occupying premises at the corner of Rosin and Hindley Streets. Hindley Street was the earliest commercial centre of Adelaide, bordered here and there by graceful little buildings designed in the late Georgian fashion. Although by 1844 Adelaide had developed considerably, ST Gill's print in that year conveys an impression of its pristine character and charm which, as the century proceeded, it was soon to lose.

To what extent Henry engaged in tailoring I do not know. In the South Australian Archives there is an account of his petitioning Colonel George Grey, the Governor at the time, protesting against the behaviour of his cutter in assaulting himself and Jane, and asking for the man's punishment. Henry's plea was rejected, on grounds not stated, but doubtless conducting a business in an embryonic, quickly growing community attracted many problems.

More interesting historically than whether Henry Downer prospered or otherwise as a tailor is the fact that during those years in Rosina Street, all his Australian children were born. First, and destined to be regarded as head of the family until his death in 1916 was Alexander George, on 28 January 1939 (by happy coincidence, my eldest child Stella Mary was born in North Adelaide on the same date one hundred and nine years later). AG, or Uncle George as he came to be known, was followed by the Downers only daughter Amelia in 1842. Then came their most celebrated son John William on 6 July 1844. Two years later, another boy appeared, Frederick Field, only to die on 2nd April 1847. Undaunted, Jane gave birth to her seventh child on 5 November 1847. He was christened Harold Field, and in the eyes of his brothers, sister and contemporaries, grew to be the most brilliant of them all.

Henry Downer forsook tailoring in 1847, and went into partnership with a Mr Graves in a general importing and wholesale grocery enterprise, trading under the caption Downer and Graves. This lasted until 1852. The firm also conducted their business in Hindley Street. But 1852 found Henry again in one of his adventurous moods. This was the year of the dramatic gold discoveries at Ballarat and Bendigo. The effect on youthful Adelaide was magnetic; half the male population made the long trek to try their luck, and amongst them was Henry Downer, taking with him his two elder boys Charles and Henry, aged eighteen and sixteen respectively. The Gold Rush was an episode when many were called but few were chosen. Our ancestor may have enjoyed the experience, but he returned home empty handed. By now, for it was 1853, his partnership with Graves had been dissolved, and he tried his hand at another venture. This time he took over a hotel, the *Blenheim*, situated like his other businesses in Hindley Street. He could not have cared for the role of a colonial entrepreneur, because in 1854 he was out of it, although between 1859 and 1860 he gave it another try. There is a bland in his activities between 1854 and 1859. By 1860, he retired from business which was probably as well since he does not seem to have displayed any commercial acumen, or an aptitude for that kind of life.

What sort of man was he? As with all the pioneers who voluntarily set out for scarcely settled, distant lands, he must have held enterprise high in his hears, and been possessed of strong courage. It seems he was a well read, indeed quite a Shakespearean scholar. His eldest son Charles, according to his daughter Marion, always spoke of him in a kindly way, saying he had plenty of ability which, in latter years, became marred by a weakness for drink. His domestic life was happy – he was certainly fortunate in his choice of a wife; he enjoyed a reputation for honest forthrightness, though perhaps inclined to be quarrelsome. He was fond of his children, although his failure to make much money curtailed his capacity to advance their interest. It was not Henry but his third son George who assisted the younger brothers with their education, and to whom they looked for guidance.

Misfortune struck at him in 1860. In the late 1850s, Jane suffered trouble from her eyes. The winged chair, with its candle sockets on each arm, in which she used to read is now in my home *Martinsell* in the Barossa ranges. Doubtless because of insufficient medical knowledge at the time, perhaps on account of a paucity of capable doctors in Adelaide, the disease assumed a more sinister aspect. Her condition worsened; the doctors called it 'Marasmus' and on the 4 January 1861, she died.

Deprived of Jane, Henry appears to have lost any ambition

for further activity. He retired to the foothills and lived in a house in a rural setting called St Bernard's near Magill. Today it no longer exists; probably it stood in what is now St Bernard's Road. There he remained throughout the 1860s until 25 September 1870 when, in the words of the press notice in Adelaide's leading daily the *Register*, he died 'after a long and painful illness in the fifty-ninth year of his age'.

The bodies of Henry and Jane, together with his mother Mary Ann and their infant son Frederick, lie in the West Terrace cemetery, Adelaide, surmounted by a tasteful Georgian memorial in stone. When the day comes for this necropolis to be returned to what Colonel Light intended, a public park for the West End of Adelaide, it is to be hoped that monuments like this will be preserved as remembrances of those who helped to create South Australia.

## The Children of Henry and Jane Downer

| | |
|---|---|
| Charles Downer | 1834–1903 |
| Henry Edward Downer MP | 1836–1905 |
| Alexander George Downer | 1839–1916 |
| Amelia Rivaz | 1842–1916 |
| The Hon Sir John William Downer KCMG, QC, MP | 1844–1915 |
| Frederick Field Downer | 1846–1847 |
| Harold Field Downer | 1847–1887 |

*Chapter 3*

# Charles Downer and his Descendants

Charles Downer was less distinguished than his brothers, but he quickly became a much-liked and esteemed member of the Adelaide community. The eldest child of Henry and Jane, he was born in England on 16 April 1834, and as we have seen, arrived with them in 1838.

His first occupation was at Port Adelaide. In 1853 or thereabouts, when only a lad of nineteen or twenty, he opened as a chemist, and lived at the Port for some years. On 19 September 1861, he married Marion Frame Hamilton in St Martin's Church, Cambelltown. She was then twenty-three, belonging to a highly regarded family, one of the founders of South Australia's wine industry. Their marriage proved happy and fruitful; in steady succession five children appeared.

Somewhat later – I do not know exactly when – Charles relinquished his business as a chemist, and became a wine and spirit merchant, trading under the name of Downer and Co, with offices in Waymouth Street. This grew into a flourishing concern, probably the principal of its kind in Adelaide.

For most of their life, the Charles Downers lived in a graceful two-storey house in Torrens Road, Kilkenny. He enjoyed outdoor sports, being a countryman at heart, though never living in the country. He was fond of horses and dogs, and in his earlier years loved hunting and coursing. Unlike his brothers, he never participated actively in public affairs despite numerous attempts to persuade him to stand for parliament. In appearance he was fairly tall, well-built and wore a moustache. His life seems to have been orderly and disciplined, evoking both respect and affection from his children. But the end came with dramatic suddenness. The morning after his sixty-ninth birthday on 17 April 1903, after a breakfast at which he seemed bright and well, he went out to look at his dogs and birds; at eleven o'clock his wife found him dead.

Charles and Marion Downer had five children. The eldest was George Henry, born on 23 July 1863. As a young man he moved to Melbourne, having qualified as a solicitor, and practised there successfully until dying in 1933. His wife was Eliza Margaret Kitchen of Melbourne whom he married in 1889. I never met him, but frequently heard him well-spoken of. The George Henry Downers in turn produced five children between 1893 and 1905 – two boys and three girls. The only one known to me was their eldest, Dr Harold Downer, who after serving with the Australian Army in the First World War, settled in England, and practised medicine at Hove, Sussex. He married a handsome and characterful Englishwoman, Claudia Clowes in 1924: they had two children, now Commander Edward Downer RN and Margaret Rosemary Downer. The Edward Downers – he married in 1947 – lived in Portsmouth, and had a son Simon George and a daughter Anne Catherine.

But to return to the offspring of Charles and Marion Downer. In 1865 their daughter Marion Jane was born. She never married, but lived until her ninetieth year, dying in August 1954. This was my cousin Marion whom I knew well ever since a very small boy. We often discussed family history. Slight of stature, tasteful in her clothes and surroundings, she embodied many Downer characteristics. Her generosity knew no bounds – indeed, she denuded herself of much of her inheritance from our uncle Alexander George in order to help her less provident relations over financial stiles, often of their own making. She was intelligent, well-read, and pungent in her comments, interested in public affairs, very definite in her views and sometimes given – as many of us have been – to intolerance. Companionship was one of her gifts, another was strong family loyalty, and although not good looking, she radiated through kindly blue eyes a sweetness of manner which proved endearing to her friends. Despite our difference in age – she was almost old enough to be my great-aunt in a normal procession of generations – we enjoyed a firm friendship, and I often think of her with affection.

There were two more sons in this particular family: Charles John and John Hamilton. The former I did not know; the latter, known as Jack, lived in Perth where I met him occasionally when passing through in the mail steamer. A fine-looking man, he spent much of his adult life in Western Australia, becoming manager of the Fremantle office of the Adelaide Steamship Company at a period when the line possessed a fleet of passenger and cargo ships. His wife Mary was ever a kind hostess, nice-looking with an understanding nature. Their daughter Ruth, so far as I know, never married; their son John farmed in the south-west of the State, and politically was an ardent supporter of the Country Party. He died in 1978.

Charles John came next in succession to Marion in the later 1860s. At first he worked in the South Australian Taxation Department, later moving to Western Australia. He married Mary Shearer about 1890; they had three boys and three girls. One of the sons, George Downer of 1892 vintage, now lives in North Adelaide with his second wife who was Miss Phyllis Gillett. Another son, Charles Hamilton, born in 1900, has managed stations for the most of his life in the north and north-east of South Australia. He is married with a son and a daughter. The third son, John, was killed in 1916 in the First World War. Each of the three girls married Victorians.

The Charles Downers named their youngest child Blanche. My youthful recollections of her as someone rather exotic, animated, untidy, a little eccentric, may be unjust. I met her rarely, and she died a long while ago. Her husband, Dr LB Blaxland of Sydney, was a descendant of the celebrated explorer. All her married life she spent in Sydney where the Blaxlands had five children, three of whom I knew. Their second daughter Alison, nicknamed Bill, married Hubert Simkins, an agreeable but idiosyncratic master of St Peter's College, Adelaide. Both she and her sister Tim, who was petite, winsome, charming and the wife of a naval officer, I used to enjoy meeting in my youth. Neither had any children, which is a loss to the world. The Blaxlands' only son was Gregory, familiarly known as Greg. He was a man of most appealing personality, with character oozing out of every pore of his skin. He served in the AIF during World War I, and again in a military capacity in the 1939–45 war. An engineer by profession, he married Helen Anderson, daughter of Brigadier-General Sir Robert Anderson of Sydney. Greg died some years ago, but many Australians have heard of his talented wife who has played such a big part in the restoration of early colonial buildings in New South Wales, and who could justly claim, were she not too modest to do so, to be a leader of decorative taste in Sydney.

A tailpiece, as it were to Gregory and Helen (now Dame Helen) Blaxland, is interesting. Their only daughter Toni married Quentin Stanham, son of Major-General Sir Reginald Stanham KCB. Lady Stanham was a MacArthur-Onslow, of historic Camden Park, New South Wales. For years now the Quentin Stanhams have lived at Camden. Not so long ago, in order to commemorate the MacArthur connection, they altered their name to MacArthur-Stanham. It is a far cry from Charles and Marion Downer to the MacArthur-Stanhams, but thus are old families from different parts of a continent linked.

*Chapter 4*

# Second Pioneer Son: HE Downer MP

~ 1 ~

Henry Edward Downer was born at Portsmouth on 22 March 1836, and was a little boy of two when he landed in South Australia with his parents and elder brother Charles in 1838. There were few schools in Adelaide in the early days; one of the best was conducted by Mr F Haire, MA, and to this he was sent. His three younger brothers George, John and Harold, followed him there. Early in life he must have set his mind on becoming a lawyer, for on leaving school, he was articled to Mr WR Wigley of the firm Wigley and Richman. In 1859 he was admitted to the Bar. The same year he married Maria Haggar at St Martin's Church, Cambelltown, a girl of unusual good looks who grew into a personality much beloved by all members of the Downer family. At this happy time he was twenty-three, she was twenty-two. Sadly, this married bliss was not to last.

Henry, however, did not remain long at the Bar, although later in life he returned to it. After five and a half years practise, he accepted a minor judicial appointment, that of Commissioner of Insolvency, where he won plaudits and distinction until 1881. Meanwhile, he and Maria made their home at Cambelltown, then a village a few miles from Adelaide at the foot of the Mt Lofty Ranges. Their place, known as 'Hilltop', had a spacious house amidst a fair acreage of land, enough for his horses of which Henry was exceedingly fond. It was here that their children were born: Ada in 1860; Alice Maria in 1862; Frank Haggar in 1863; Harold Charles in 1865; Lottie Amelia in

1869. Each of them emerged as people of great quality, except Lottie who only survived until 1872.

By the beginning of the 1880s, Henry had become attracted to politics. This, of course, entailed relinquishing the Commissionership of Insolvency which he did in 1881, returning to the Bar in partnership with his youngest brother Harold. That year he was elected MP for Encounter bay in the South Australian Parliament. By this time, his brother John had not only been a member for three years, but was about to become Attorney-General in the Bray ministry, so in the House of Assembly, John and Henry were the first two brothers to sit simultaneously in that body. Henry held the seat – it was a two-member constituency – until 1896, during which time he proved an energetic representative of his district. For example, to him and his colleague, Simpson Newland, belongs the credit of converting the horse tramway from Strathalbyn to Victor Harbour into a railway service – maybe a small matter in terms of achievement viewed from nearly a century later, but just the sort of issue which always excited lively interest, mixed with contention, in the minds of electors. More significant was his crusade in parliament for improvements to the Law of Insolvency, based on his long experience in the Insolvency Court. Largely through his efforts, the Distress for Rent Act was passed in 1888, by which the law was altered in important respects, particularly in restricting a landlord to taking only the goods of his tenants for rent.

Fortune smiled brightly on Henry in 1890, if only briefly. On 2 May he became Attorney-General in Dr John Cockburn's government. He was not long enough in office to make his mark as a minister, for the following August, the administration was defeated by Thomas Playford, grandfather of the State's longest serving Premier. Unhappily, he was never to regain high office. And the following year he received another rebuff from Playford, who by now had become his enemy.

The episode is related by AJ Hannan QC in his scholarly

life of Chief Justice Way. In 1891, Way, who by then had been Chief Justice for fifteen years, and had just been appointed Lieutenant-Governor by the British Government to the surprise of Playford and his Cabinet, recommended to the Governor-in-Council that Henry Edward Downer be appointed a Queen's Counsel. There could be little argument as to Henry's qualifications. By then he had been a barrister for thirty-two years, a local court judge for sixteen years, and for a short while Attorney-General of the State. Playford objected on personal grounds. He declared that Henry had constantly attacked him, and behaved very unfairly to him. Consequently, he could not bring himself to make the recommendation to the Governor. The Governor at that time was the Earl of Kintore, a staunch friend of the Downer family, especially my father and later on my eldest half-brother John. He argued with Playford that the Chief Justice's recommendation should be accepted. The ministers supported Playford; no appointment was made. By this time, Way had sailed on furlough for England, leaving Sir James Boucaut as Acting Chief Justice. Subsequently, the cabinet seemingly relented to the extent that they informed Boucaut that Way's recommendation would be considered after he returned from England. But no further recommendation was made, perhaps because Way – who on the Bench prided himself in never having a judgment upset on appeal – did not wish to risk further charging. Thus was Henry denied an accolade highly prized by every member at the Bar.

Was this his own fault? Perhaps he may have contributed by his opposition to Playford's policies by a mounting dislike of Playford himself. Politicians are an assembly of incongruities; few succeed without ambition. In every parliament under the sun, in every party, men arouse strong antipathies, not so much from the clash of policies, as from being on differing wavelengths. An exalted mind can soar above personal discords, and when confronted by a choice of recognising publicly an opponent's merit or denying him his desserts, accord the adversary his due. This is the real criticism of Playford's meanness. A bigger man, however provoked he might have felt, would have accepted the Chief Justice's recommendation, and the Governor's persuasions, and given Henry an honour which he had earned professionally and which had little to do with politics.

Nevertheless, there were compensations. Henry was a rounded man, with many interests apart from politics and the law. He enjoyed life and lived it to the full. Foremost was his love of horses and hunting. From his youth he had been an adept horseman and for decades was an ardent rider to hounds. There was probably no more prominent member of the Adelaide Hunt Club in the nineteenth century: twice he became Master. It was no accident that both his sons, Frank and Charles, were almost, as it were, born in the saddle, and in their own generation, as we shall see, became equally accomplished. Nor did he and his family live entirely at *Hilltop*. Towards the middle of the 1880s, his brother John sold him part of the *Glenalta Estate*, then unspoilt country near the eastern slopes of Mount Lofty. Here he built a pleasant stone house which he named *Nara*, set amidst stately white Gums and with enough grazing land for his purposes. Every summer the Henry Downers would move to *Nara*, barely ten minutes walk across the paddocks from *Glenalta*. There, at an altitude of 1500 feet, they relaxed in one of the best summer climates in the world.

Henry engaged in other activities of a public-spirited nature. For the greater part of his life he participated in Freemasonry, being almost singular in my family to do so. Prior to the establishment of the Grand Lodge of South Australia, he was Deputy District Grand Master for about fourteen years under the English Constitution. Then, when the Grand Lodge was set up in 1884, he was unanimously elected Deputy Grand Master. He was also closely associated with the organisation of the Anglican Church, holding various parochial offices, and being a member of the Synod. Whether in himself he found profound religious beliefs I do not know; as with most of us, there are indications that on occasions he found the Christian ideal hard to fulfil; but he certainly was a man of faith, and steadfast in his support of the Church as an entity. I think, too, that he was proud of being a pioneer, through only a child when he arrived. He appears in group photographs at an Old Colonists Dinner in 1871, bearing a strong resemblance to some of us of later generations.

Henry lived until his seventieth year. In 1903, after a bout of ill-health, he visited England and Japan, but sea air and other countries fail to improve his conditions. By then he was suffering from asthma; this worsened on his return. After an illness of thirteen weeks, he finally succumbed on 4 August 1905. He was buried at Cambelltown, where Maria followed him seven years later. Many tributes were paid to him, in parliament, in the courts, in the organisations which he helped, and by his innumerable friends drawn from all walks of life. The *Advertiser*, in a long and warm obituary outlining his career and his interests described him as 'one of the best known men in Adelaide'.

~ 2 ~

This is a convenient place to say something of Henry and Maria Downer's children, and of their descendants, with the exception of Frank H Downer who deserves a chapter to himself.

Ada, their eldest, was born on 22 November, 1860. She grew up to be a tall, good-looking woman, with graceful bearing, a most kindly disposition, showing considerable style in her houses and her clothes. Opportunity came her way in 1887 when her uncle, Sir John, then Premier of South Australia, asked her to accompany him and his wife to the first Colonial Conference in London. This enabled her to catch glimpses of English life on the grand scale, when Britain was at the height of her wealth, influence and power in the world. In 1892 in Adelaide, she married Otto Heinrick Schomburgk, son of Dr

Richard von Schomburgk, a noted German botanist whom the South Australian Government induced to found the Adelaide Botanical Gardens in 1866. There is a street named after him in Canberra. The Schomburgks were an old Saxony family with aristocratic connections in Holland. As a boy and young man, I often met my cousin Ada, who always exuded an interest in what I was doing, and genuine charm; she was one of my family favourites. Otto, for years, was Sheriff of the Adelaide Gaol: rotund in face, bald in later life, somewhat corpulent in body, he seemed the incarnation of all the better German qualities. He must have treated the prisoners benignly – even though his duties compelled him to witness executions – with his courteous manners and habitual generosity. As a host, he was all that a boy with a healthy appetite could hope for: when you dined with the Schomburgks, you were regaled with a succession of delicately cooked courses and appropriate wines which gave as much delight to the young as embarrassment to the elderly. They lived first on South Terrace and in the last phase of their lives in Grove Street, Unley Park, with a cottage in the Hills near Nara and Glenalta, as an escape from Adelaide's hot summers. Several times they journeyed to England and the Continent, and for long periods, as their eldest daughter Pauline lived at Windermere. Once they visited Germany to the delight of Otto's relations who feted their kinsfolk from such a far-away country. Ada died in 1941, retaining her prettiness to the last; Otto two or three years before.

The Schomburgks had three children: Pauline, born in 1893, who married Jock Spedding Curwen, soldier and architect, a scion of a Westmoreland family settled in the English Lakes District for centuries. Their second daughter, Alice Marie, known as Molly, followed in 1897. In 1919 she married John G Howard on his return to Adelaide from the First World War. They in turn had two sons, one of whom, Richard Howard, is a skilful maker of wrought iron. Ada and Otto's son, Richard Henry, dates from 1899. He also served in the First World War, subsequently marrying Jean Moyes of Adelaide. They have two daughters and a son Ian who, with his English wife, lives in England.

The Henry Downers' second daughter was named Alice Maria, who lived a long and happy life from 1862 until 1960. Like her sister Ada, she was tall with finely chiselled features, and endowed with a stately poise, a carefully articulated musical voice, together with a personality impressive in its unaffected dignity. Occasionally vague but always deeply religious, she applied her beliefs to innumerable worthy causes, and privately helped many in less fortunate circumstances, often at real sacrifice to herself about which she never complained. She married twice, the first time Charles H Warren in 1891, and again in the mid 1920s Bruce Rudall, then a retired solicitor from Gawler. After Charles Warren died, she lived in her father's house, *Nara,* where she extended the garden to a scene of tranquil, rambling, woodland beauty. It was here that, well into her sixties, she brought her old school friend Bruce Rudall, himself a widower, to live with her.

The Warrens were an early South Australian pastoral family. The original home, *Springfield*, near Williamstown has now been transformed by the present owners, Mr and Mrs Byron MacLachlan, into one of Australia's most beautiful country seats. Alice and Charles had two daughters. The eldest, Jean, Lady Bonython was so well-known that her manifold activities deserve a book of their own. She quickly became one of the most remarkable feminine personalities of twentieth century Adelaide. In her adolescence she married Lavington Bonython in 1912, during his initial term as Mayor of Adelaide (the city was not elevated to a lord mayoralty until 1925). Apart from acquiring three step-children – Sir Lavington's first wife was a daughter of Sir John Bray, one of my father's political colleagues – she proceeded to have three children of her own. Charles Warren, her first-born has inherited much of his parents' flair for public service as well as being a latter-day explorer; her daughter, christened Katherine Downer, now lives appropriately at *Nara* with her husband, Colin Verco; the youngest son, Hugh Reskymer, known as Kym, operates as a flashing meteor of human vitality in Sydney and Adelaide.

My cousin Alice and Charlie Warren had another daughter, Kathleen Mary, born in 1892. All her life she has been called Bobbie; I doubt whether even her closest friends would recognise the names on her birth certificate. In appearance and temperament she has closely resembled her mother, with the same tall stature, the equally musical intonation, the same grace and quiet charm. After the First World War she married an officer in the P&O, Hugh Codrington-Forsyth, a descendant of one of Nelson's admirals. Theirs was an old-fashioned shipboard romance. They met on a voyage from Australia to England, married, had two children and lived happily ever after. Hugh Forsyth eventually rose to be Commodore of the P&O fleet. Since his death, Bobbie continues to live in England where she and Hugh found so much happiness beginning in the 1920s.

I have said earlier that the Henry Downers' sons were named Frank and Harold Charles. Charles was born on 24 August 1865 at *Hilltop*, Cambelltown. He gained his early education at the Hahndorf Academy, and then proceeded to St Peter's College where he excelled in sport. For a number of years he was acclaimed the best hurdle-racer in the State, but his prowess was not confined to athletics. On leaving school, he went into the Engineer-in-Chief's office, but being a countryman in spirit, preferred a life on the land. For some time he managed *Melton*, the station of his uncle Alexander George Downer, and after further experience acquired, a property of his own near Strathalbyn. Later he moved to a farm at Saddleworth, having meanwhile acquired a town house at Walkerville. In 1909 he married Bertha Law-Smith, one of the daughters of the well-known Adelaide merchant Richard Smith. Their only son, Tom, born in 1913, has made his mark as will appear hereafter.

As with his brother Frank, Charlie Downer excelled as a rider, and was a prominent member of the Adelaide Hunt Club. Few could equal his skill on the polo field; physically strong, he lacked a robust constitution, and died far too young in 1921 aged fifty-six. Perhaps his most fitting epitaph came from the *Advertiser*:

> He was widely known and highly esteemed for his many manly qualities. He was a staunch friend, a man who scorned meanness and one who was the soul of honour in all his dealings with his fellows.

## *Chapter 5*

# Family Head: Alexander George Downer

It is unusual for the third son of a large family to be regarded by his own and succeeding generations and the principal member, but such was the position of our benefactor Uncle George. The first Downer to be born in South Australia on 28 January 1839, he was destined for a long, varied and highly successful life which ended amidst the convulsions of the First World War in 1916.

George followed his brother Henry to Mr Haire's school, and as with Henry, developed a liking for the law. On leaving school, he became articled to the legal firm of Bartley, Bakewell, & Stow where he quickly displayed an aptitude for his chosen profession. As his studies expanded, he became attracted to journalism, and for a while edited the *Telegraph* which had the historical distinction of being the first penny newspaper in Australia. This venture, however, he did not pursue for long. He decided to concentrate on his first love, the law, and in 1868 was admitted to the South Australian Bar. His younger brother John had commenced practice the year before, so they immediately formed a partnership: G & J Downer, which rapidly became one of the most celebrated legal firms in the State. In those days, as now, the two branches of the profession were combined. My father from the start preferred the forensic side in which he soon excelled; George for his part concentrated on commercial law and the general practice of a solicitor. They were a remarkable combination, each containing qualities which the other lacked, yet united by a depth of friendship seldom surpassed between brothers. For the rest of the century, and in the earlier years of the twentieth century, many of the *causes celebres* of South Australian legal history were fought from their office in King William Street.

George Downer's interest in commercial law naturally led him through the gateway to commerce. He seems to have been born with an instinct for finance and flourishing enterprise. As soon as he acquired sufficient capital, he invested in land; in sites on the growing city of Adelaide, in stations in the scarcely developed northern and north-eastern parts of the State, in hotels which he saw would acquire high value as real estate, in rural property close to Adelaide such as Belair near where he established his country house *Monalta* surrounded by hundreds of acres of apple orchards and grazing land. His principal station was *Melton* in the north-east, which he owned until his death, and it was on vast estates such as these that more than one of his nephews gained valuable experience.

Ability as a lawyer, his uncanny financial judgment, his progressive nature and his general perspicacity caused him to be much sought after by leading Adelaide companies. In 1889, he joined the board of the Bank of Adelaide; by 1894 he was chairman, a position he retained until his retirement in 1914. In 1892 he became a director of Elder Smith & Company, where he likewise remained until poor health forced his general withdrawal from professional and business activity. About this time, he became chairman of the China Traders Company, and joined the board of Norwich Union Assurance. On each of these bodies, his legal knowledge, shrewdness and brilliance as a financier proved of inestimable benefit in the eyes of his contemporaries.

As with other members of his family, Uncle George had a taste for good living. Whilst yet a young man, he established his home on South Terrace in the early 1860s. Later he acquired his Belair estate, which he named *Monalta* where he spent the summer months and gradually more and more of whatever spare time he had. He never married; why, I do not know. Not that he lacked sociability, or eschewed the company of women. On the contrary, he enjoyed giving parties, was a courtly, gracious and genial host and he rejoiced in friendship. One of his closest friends was Peter Waite, chairman of Elder Smith, the founder of the great agricultural research institute on the foothills of Mount Lofty which bears his name, and like George a pioneer pastoralist and commercial leader of extraordinary capacity. For long years each would take it in turns to call on the other every Sunday morning, either at *Urrbrae* or *Monalta*. Another friend and business colleague was Robert Barr Smith, one of South Australia's most illustrious names, whose great-granddaughter it was my supreme happiness to marry in 1947.

Yet it was a family life that lay at the core of George Downer's existence. His father, lacking in capacity to make money or seize the infinite possibilities of prospering in the infant colony, George took it upon himself at the beginning of the 1860s after Henry Downer's retirement, to assume the mantle of paterfamilias. He assisted his youngest brother Harold with educational expenses, sent him to Cambridge thence to Paris. He became counsellor and frequent financial help to his older brothers, sister and their children. As the decades progressed, his advice was sought on nearly every conceivable problem. One of his nephews or nieces, I forget which, was diagnosed as suffering from appendicitis. Was an operation necessary? Yes, urged the surgeon. No, said Uncle George. There was no operation, and no ill consequences.

His generosity was widespread. For his sister Amelia, in her widowhood, he bought a house and garden in Molesworth Street, North Adelaide, where she lived until her death and where afterwards her daughter Florrie dwelt until her own demise in 1947. For his nephew Harold Rivaz, he made available his house at Brighton. My half-brother John was established on a property known as *Hawthorndene*, close to the National Park – a district since reduced through faulty planning to tightly packed suburbia. Other indigent relations were similarly favoured. So were many friends.

Outside the family, he assisted innumerable charitable causes without publicity or ostentation. But despite his early essays into journalism, he shunned self-advertisement and was devoid of any sense of what nowadays would be termed public relations. He was seldom photographed; his portrait was never painted; very few impressions of him of any kind exist. Politics as such made no appeal to him, except in his youth when, at the beginning of the 1870s he contested unsuccessfully the House of Assembly seat of Gumeracha, which he left to his brothers Sir John and Henry. He was always prepared to advise governments if they sought his opinion, such as when he served on a pastoral commission in the 1880s; but generally he preferred to stand behind the scenes.

What were his recreations? He shared a love of horses with his brothers and older nephews – horses and carriages, after all, for most of his life were the chief means of private transport. He enjoyed the turf, kept his own racing stables, and was seldom happier than when a nephew, such as Frank, would ride on one of his horses to victory. On Easter Monday, his drag was a customary sight at Oakbank. Travel seems to have enticed him less than the rest of us. He visited England and the continent at least twice, the first time in the late 1860s, but showed no disposition to move far afield in his later days. As with all Downers, he was proud of his British ancestry, and displayed a warm attachment to things British. There is a long story that at one period he contemplated leaving much of his fortune to the British government, an aberration of mind which, mercifully for most of us, soon passed. But it illustrates the genuineness of his sentiments.

My recollection of Uncle George is that of a child, when my father occasionally took me to *Monalta*. This was towards the end of his life when clearly a small boy pretending to be a steam-engine irritated him. Of medium height, with broad shoulders like his brothers, he wore a carefully trimmed beard. In his clothes he was immaculate, preferring the late Victorian and Edwardian fashions of a long frock-coat surmounted by varieties of top hats. His head bore all the signs of an able man: a deep brow, a thrust in the back, balanced proportions. At home he loved his garden and above all his dogs for which he had a passion. If he had one he must have had half a dozen, in my time Australian terriers. He was not a collector of fine furniture or silver, but his pictures revealed an eclectic taste ranging from Old Masters to early twentieth century Australian. Three of his pictures hang in my home, *Martinsell*; another is in the Adelaide Gallery. His contemporaries spoke of his polished manners, his sense of humour, and an unselfishness which characterised his whole life. Even more praiseworthy was his reputation for integrity, forthrightness, and straight dealing. And at his christening, the fairies bestowed on him that priceless gift of worldly success: good judgment.

By 1914 George Downer, aged seventy-five, felt he had had enough. He was in indifferent health, and considered he should make way for younger men. Accordingly, in May he resigned from all his directorates and virtually ceased his legal practice. Such was his standing in the South Australian community that the *Advertiser* wrote a special article to signalise the occasion. Part of it is worth quoting as illustrating how he appeared in an era of world history which was just about to close:

> Although Mr Downer never enjoyed parliamentary honours, he has been associated on so many different points, and in so influential a manner with the mercantile life of South Australia that in every sense but the political, he may be viewed as a public man, and one too of such eminence and distinction that his place will not be readily filled. The members of the Downer family as lawyers, politicians, and men of affairs have all in various directions left a creditable mark upon the history of the State, but none has more honourably discharged the duties of citizenship, or with a higher measure of ability … He has played with remarkable success … a series of parts calling for versatile talent of no common order, and he has done so in such a

> manner as not merely to win for himself material rewards of unflagging industry and keen intelligence, but to gain the confidence of all with whom he has been associated in business, and a respect of the whole community.

The tribute then refers to his pioneering work in the pastoral industry and continues:

> In his profession, Mr Downer has attained special distinction as an authority on commercial law. To the companies on which he has acted as director his legal knowledge has been of considerable service, but he became well-nigh indispensable to them because of the unusual combination of valuable qualities among which may be noted a spirit of enterprise and progressiveness duly teamed with the wisest prudence …

Retirement was not protracted, and it was clouded with sorrows. He was frequently unwell despite the bracing air and picturesque landscape of *Monalta*. He had always assumed that his younger brother, friend, and partner Sir John would survive him, and play a predominant part in the administration of his Will. These hopes were belied when my father died in August the following year. A fortnight later he suffered a severe heart attack, occasioned no doubt by this sad event. In July 1916, his only sister Amelia died. George by now was the sole remnant of his generation. He had always disliked August: it had never been for him a lucky month. His brothers Henry and John, then Amelia, had died in August. Now it was his turn. Without any regrets, life having lost its purpose, he expired on 17 August 1916 in his seventy-eighth year.

Many tributes ensued. The *Advertiser* headlined his passing: 'A Splendid Citizen'. Linking him with Sir John, that newspaper wrote:

> They have left a record of excellent work done for the community, and memories rendered fragrant by their gentleness, courtesy, and high attainments. Few men commanded greater public respect or attracted more

> personal friends than Sir John Downer and his brother. They were personifications of all that wins affection and good repartee in political or commercial circles. There was an indescribable charm about their dispositions which was irresistible … Mr George Downer had no taste for legislative work but he was a prominent figure in the commercial world where his tact, keenness, and suavity were proverbial. He had perfect control both of his temper and his judgment on all occasions, and he was an ideal Chairman of a Board meeting or a gathering of shareholders … He was transparently honest and sincere. That was the secret of his popularity. There was no member of the legal profession more generally respected and admired by clients and the community at large.

Among Uncle George's relations, however, there were assuagements to grief. His qualities of mind, during a long life, had amassed a considerable fortune. Probate of his will was granted for £400,000–£800,000 in the present currency. At today's debased values, this sum would be worth four or five times that amount. After charitable bequests, he directed that the bulk of his estate be divided between his fourteen nephews and nieces. For years afterwards, realisations of the other portions of his estate added substantially to the original total. In this way, more than any other member of the family – none of the other brothers died rich men – he must be regarded as the principal architect of the Downer material fortunes. As his youngest nephew I salute him, and will ever praise his name.

## *Chapter 6*

# Amelia 1842–1916

Amelia is an entr'acte in the nineteenth century Downer saga. She was the only girl amongst six brothers, and as such occupied a special place in the family when young. Her birthday was 5 July 1842: she lived for seventy-four years.

I know little about her early life. Opportunities for a display of talents would have been slight for a girl amidst the restrictions and conventions of the early Victorian age, growing up in a sparsely populated colony a few years after its foundation. She married when quite young, probably in 1863. Her husband was Arthur Rivaz, eleven years her senior. Of his origins all I have heard is that he belonged to a long-established Spanish family, and that he came to South Australia in 1853, a young man of twenty-two. Their two surviving offspring certainly displayed a strong Spanish streak in their appearance.

For most of his early years in the colony, Arthur worked on the sheep and cattle stations of Mr John Baker, father of Sir Richard. In 1868 he joined the Civil Service, spending seven years in the offices of the Local Court, and the next three years in the Lands Title Office. In 1876 he displayed alarming symptoms of heart disease, so much so that Dr Corbin warned him he might live only another two years. Hopefully, in company with the HE Downers, he and Amelia sailed for England, but after their return, the doctor's melancholy foreboding was fulfilled. Whilst staying with his brother-in-law George Downer at *Monalta*, he died on 8 August 1872.

Amelia's life with Arthur was happy but chequered. In 1864 Arthur Henry was born; he lived until only twenty-three. Their second boy Frederick, born in 1865, died the following year, eighteen-months old. Their third son, Harold George was more fortunate: he enjoyed a full life-span despite lameness in one of his legs, married a sympathetic, kind and capable woman Annabel Sinclair, although was denied the gift of children. Then came two daughters, Nellie and Florrie.

When misfortune struck again in 1873, with Arthur Rivaz's death, Amelia became a widow at thirty-six with four children to bring up. As in all the family's troubles, the redoubtable Uncle George threw a protective shield around her, contributing much to her well-being and the children's education. She never married again.

My recollection of Aunt Amelia is only a child's impression of an invalid. Whenever I went to her home in Molesworth Street, North Adelaide, the old lady lay propped up in bed with asthma, bronchitis or some other ailment. During the last years of her life she suffered greatly in health, and this ailed to earlier sorrows and affected her temperament. But long before this decline she acquired a reputation for keen sensitivity, quick to take offence at imaginary slights, a personality her relations learnt through experience required handling with care. In this delicate exercise my mother was not always successful, although she tried very hard.

There was another extenuating circumstance for Amelia's difficult ways. In her eldest daughter Nellie, the family had cause for pride. Elegant, vivacious, beautiful, she married an English army officer, Major Russel, whose regiment was stationed in India – and in India, of course, they lived. Only a few years after their marriage, on a voyage home to England by P & O, Nellie developed acute appendicitis. Whilst the ship was in the Mediterranean she died, being buried at sea. A bitter blow to poor Amelia who, before reaching sixty, had lost her husband, two of her sons and now her talented daughter.

Of Amelia's surviving children, Florrie was the one I knew best. Only rarely with Harold Rivaz did our paths cross.

Lacking progeny of his own, he and his wife adopted a baby who they named Jock. Jock married a pretty Adelaide girl, Roma Blades, and their handsome son David is the husband of Robina Barr Smith, Sir Tom Barr Smith's youngest daughter.

My cousin Florrie deserves more than a passing reference. She was one of the most vital, animated, and downright uncompromising of all my relations. She could never have been beautiful, although her straight nose, slim figure, wood stature, dark flashing eyes inherited no doubt from her Spanish antecedents, all combined to produce a presence which, when roused, was intimidating. As a daughter she fulfilled the fifth commandment to her mother both in duty and in love. She never married, yet in her youth her opportunities must have been many. Her kindness of heart seemed unending, especially to her relatives. As a small boy, equally as a man, it was always a pleasure to call on her in Molesworth Street – once you had escaped the attentions of her aggressive pet magpies in the garden. She would receive you in her small morning room discoursing over tea and cakes served from a gate-legged table about events and people, always with pronounced emphasis. After Aunt Amelia died in 1916, an old friend Olive Stow came to live with her: this arrangement lasted most happily for the remainder of her life. Together they became inveterate travellers, principally to England where Florrie had made many friends. Faithful to her headquarters at the Vanderbilt Hotel, South Kensington – a superior hotel in the inter-war decades to what it is now – Florrie visited London repeatedly, saw every theatre of interest (she would not have been amused by *Oh Calcutta!*), revelled in the incomparable English and Scottish countryside, and occasionally made a cautious foray to the continent. Wherever one encountered her, whether it was Adelaide, Melbourne, London or Oxford, she was always the same emphatic, vibrant spirit. Victorian in her standards, she contrived to remain perpetually young because of her absorption of the changing world around her and her concern for the welfare of others. She lived until January 1947. As she lay dying, I told her of my engagement to Mary Gosse. I believe by the warmth of her response that she was sufficiently conscious to realise these joyous tidings for our family.

## *Chapter 7*

# The Hon Sir John Downer KCMG, QC, MP 1844–1915

In the person of John William Downer the family attained a high water mark which has not yet been exceeded. He was born on 6 July 1844 at a time when South Australia was recovering from a severe economic crisis. Adelaide's population numbered little more than 6000; there were barely 18,000 people in the entire colony. Administration was conducted by the Governor, Captain George Grey, assisted by a Council of four official members, and four members nominated by himself. The former comprised the Governor, the Colonial Secretary AM Mundy, the Advocate-General W Smillie, and the Colonial Treasurer Captain Sturt. The non-official Councillors were Major TS O'Halloran, Jacob Hagen, John Morphett and Captain Charles H Bagot. In England, since 1841, the Conservatives had captured power with Sir Robert Peel as Prime Minister. This was the political framework of the Province and the other Country into which the baby destined to become a notable Australian statesman emerged.

His early education followed the course of this elder brothers Henry and George at the school of Mr F Haire. From there he proceeded to St Peter's College at the close of the 1850s, having first won a scholarship open to all boys in the State. St Peter's, though founded in 1847, assumed its recognisable form two years later; by the time young John went to it the School House as exiting today had been erected only four or five years before. His career there was brilliant, and he owed something to the warm encouragement he received from Dr GH Farr, the Headmaster. In Greek, Latin, English, he achieved high distinction, as his prizes show; another prize for Diligence, provides an index to his success in life. By the time he left school, at the close of 1861, he was acknowledged as the outstanding scholar in the State, as was shown by his gaining first place in a public examination.

John then embraced the law as a profession, along with Henry, who by 1859 was practising, and George. There was no university in Adelaide until 1874, so the only way to the Bar was to become articled. This he did with Mr Rupert Ingleby, gaining admission on 23 March 1867. Next year, as we have seen, he joined forces with Alexander George, and thus came into being GJ Downer, Barristers and Solicitors, with John concentrating on court work.

In 1869 his life nearly ended. Whilst out hunting in the vicinity of Marrogate in the eastern Mount Lofty Ranges, he fell from his horse, injuring his head severely. His companions carried him to a shepherd's cottage where he lay unconscious for days. Gradually his strength returned, assisted by the ministrations of Dr Esau from Woodside, but a slight scar on his forehead remained forever.

His rise at the bar was rapid. Within ten years, at the extraordinarily young age of thirty-four, he took silk. Before that, he had made his first voyage to England; more important, in 1871 he married. His bride was Miss Elizabeth Henderson, the daughter of a Presbyterian minister, the Reverend James Henderson whose responsibilities then lay in the Mount Barker district. They were much of an age, she being two years younger. Their first boy, John Henry, was born the following year; then came James Frederick in 1874. They had a third boy, Harold Sydney, in 1875 but he died a week before Christmas in 1876. During this period John and Elizabeth – she was known in the family as Lizzie – lived in Gilles Street, near East Terrace. In appearance tall, well-groomed, she looks handsome in her photographs rather than beautiful. My relations all spoke about her with affection, as did my half-brother Fred. She was intelligent, witty though sometimes incisive, kind and companionable. It was a happy marriage, sadly foreshortened by her premature death.

The year 1878 not only saw JW Downer being made a QC, but becoming a member of parliament. On 11 April he was elected to the House of Assembly, then a body of forty-six in number, for the district of Barossa. The constituencies in those days were larger than now; for example, Gawler, for which he did so much, was its principal town, and were represented by two members. His colleague was Dr Martin Basedow until 1890, and then Mr James Haigh. Barossa extended through Tanunda, Nuriootpa, Angaston, across the ranges down to the Murray plains. In the last quarter of the nineteenth century many of the inhabitants sprang from pioneer German colonists who settled in South Australia between 1838 and 1845. Fortunately for us, they preserved their national customs, architecture, even their language. But this involved difficulties when it came to communicating, unless one spoke German which my father did not. So in his campaigns he at first used to take an interpreter. Later on, when the district was unswervingly his, he would on appropriate occasions vary speech making by piano performances at which he was adept, garnished by sons. No doubt his skill as an amateur musician coupled with histrionic ability and a keen sense of humour compensated somewhat for his linguistic deficiency.

After his election to Parliament, though not because of it (the financial rewards were slight indeed), John Downer elevated his style of living. In 1880 he purchased his home on Pennington Terrace, what is now St Mark's College. In those days it was numbered 42, without a name, nor did he give it one. It was a well-constructed, two-storey house in the Victorian manner, built only a few years before, to which he added a ballroom forming an entresol floor entered from a landing on the main staircase, and a spacious billiard room half underground – a cool refuge in Adelaide summers when air conditioning was not yet a visionary's dream. I think he was fond of Pennington Terrace, as he used to refer to it, although he once described it as a cross between a privy and a palace. At any rate, he was to live there for the remaining thirty-five years of his life, and inside its walls were staged significant events in Australian history.

The same year he also bought what was then a country property in the Mount Lofty Ranges, near Carey Gully. It was part of the considerable *Woodhouse Estate* of the late Sir Richard Hanson, a distinguished Chief Justice and scholar who had died in 1876. *Glenalta*, as John named it, was then a cottage built of pise in 1863 with a picturesque shingle roof. I have an idea he discovered this enchanting spot in the late 1870s when out riding, and at first leased it. Whether this is so or not, after acquiring *Glenalta*, he built a new single storey house of Mount Lofty stone attached to the original dwelling, and in this form it remained until 1935 when his eldest surviving son Fred placed a second floor over the main part of the house, at the same time demolishing the earlier pise rooms. From 1880 onward, my father and his family would retire to *Glenalta* from early December until April, and in this beautiful valley, then peaceful, remote, undisturbed by its cruel fate nearly a century later of freeway and creeping suburbia, he planted many of the splendid English trees one sees today.

Once in Parliament, his ascension was as rapid as at the Bar. He quickly became one of the best debaters in the House, earning respect and friendship from supporters and opponents alike. On 24 June 1881, forty-three years to the day after his parents landed in South Australia, he became Attorney-General in the Government led by John Bray. His colleagues at first were Alfred Catt, J Langdon Parsons, L Glyde, and JG Ramsay; in March 1884 Parsons having been appointed Government Resident of the Northern Territory (at that time part of South Australia) his place was taken by Sir Edwin Smith, whilst in April David Bower succeeded Glyde. During his three years in office, John Downer, displaying the reforming zeal of a young man – he was not yet thirty-seven when given his first portfolio – effected important legal reforms. Chief of these were his Married Women's Property Bill under which a married woman was allowed to retain her own property; the granting to accused persons the right to give evidence on their own behalf; and amendments to the law of insolvency, and marriage. Such liberalisation of the law evoked warm plaudits from both public opinion and the press.

The Bray Government fell in June 1884 almost exactly three years after its formation. A year out of office gave John his biggest opportunity. Bray had gone for a sojourn in England, leaving John as Leader of the Opposition. Twelve months later he carried a no-confidence notion against the Colton Government. The Governor, Sir William Robinson, sent for him, requesting him to form an administration. Thus on 16 June 1885, at the age of forty, he became one of the youngest Premiers South Australia has known.

The first Downer Ministry was composed as follows:

| | |
|---|---|
| Premier and Attorney-General: | JW Downer QC |
| Treasurer (until 1885): | Simpson Newland |
| Chief Secretary (until 1886): | JB Spence |
| Commissioner for Public Works (until October 1885): | John Darling |
| Commissioner for Grown Lands: | JH Howe |
| Minister for Education and Agriculture: | Dr John A Cockburn |

After Simpson Newland retired in 1886, Sir John Bray replaced him as Treasurer. That same year, when Mr Spence resigned, Mr David Murray became Chief Secretary. Simpson Newland, besides his interest in politics, was a pioneer pastoralist, the author of the best-seller *Paving the Way*, and the father of one of Australia's great surgeons Sir Henry Newland. John Darling is better remembered as the founder of a notable firm of grain merchants with world-wide connections, John

Darling & Son. His grandson, Harold Darling, was chairman of Broken Hill Proprietary Limited in the 1930s and 1940s. David Murray, a commercial leader in the late nineteenth century Adelaide, established with his brother, the well known business of D & A Murray. Dr Cockburn, later Sir John, subsequently headed a ministry of his own, and eventually proceeded to London as Agent-General. Mr Howe became a delegate to the Federal Conventions in the 1890s.

The administration, though made up of men of talent and expertise, did not have any easy passage. Simpson Newland proved rather a reluctant Treasurer. Darling returned after merely four months. The Government's principal achievement was to enact a modest measure of tariff protection for local industries. In their first year, over half a million pounds of loan money was voted for railways; about the same on waterworks; lesser sums for defence, harbour improvements, telegraph and telephone services. In 1886 the Cabinet was reconstructed. Bray, back from England, returned to office; Newland departed; David Murray took Spence's place. Another loan bill of £850,000 provided for £450,000 to be spent on improvements to pastoral leases, a further £200,000 on water conservation, £125,000 for Beetaloo waterworks. Legislation was passed concerning real property, gold-mining, and other matters. Of greater significance to the future of the State was the agreement the Premier personally concluded with WB Chaffey, from California, for the inauguration of the Murray irrigation settlements at Renmark, twenty-five miles from the Victorian border. Chaffey's earlier negotiations with the Victorian Government had broken down; my father quickly seized the opportunity to attract him to the South Australian Murray, and so came into being Renmark which in turn led to other irrigation areas further downstream. Having represented this district myself in the Australian Parliament between 1949 and 1964, this is one of my father's achievements which gives me especial cause for pride.

It was during the first Downer administration that a big step forward occurred in inter-colonial communications. By 1886 work on the extension of the railway line from Murray Bridge to the Victorian border station of Serviceton reached completion. This enabled passenger and freight transport to Melbourne. The first Melbourne to Adelaide express drew into the central railway station on North Terrace on 21 January, thus inaugurating the daily service which has continued ever since. For most South Australians, the Melbourne express must have seemed a boon. However slow or uncomfortable those gas-lit carriages in retrospect seem to us, they presented to travellers in the 1880s a quicker alternative to the two days voyage from Port Adelaide to the Yarra in small steamers along a coastline which is very often rough.

The Government, too, devoted a good deal of attention to organising the Jubilee Exhibition to commemorate the fiftieth anniversary of South Australia's foundation. Much contention surrounded these plans, which eventually were realised through the determination of Sir Edwin Smith and Sir Samuel Davenport. A special Exhibition Building arose on North Terrace, demolished only in the 1960s to make way for what is now the Napier Building of the Adelaide University. As ill luck would have it, the Exhibition was not opened until 21 June 1887, a few days after the Ministry's defeat whilst Sir John (as he had now become) was overseas.

In 1886 a rare opportunity, of far more historical importance than anything I have related, came to the youthful Premier. Arrangements were set in motion by Downing Street to convoke a Colonial Conference during the English spring of 1887 as a feature of Queen Victoria's Jubilee celebrations. This was to be attended by prime ministers or representatives of all self-governing states throughout the British Empire. It was John Downer's first chance to play a part on the world stage; urged on by his Cabinet colleagues, he took it. With his wife Elizabeth, and one of his nieces Ada Downer, they sailed from Glenelg on 29 January in the P & O liner *Sutlej* of 4200 tons, one of the newer ships on the run. He had interesting travelling companions: Deakin, then Chief Secretary of Victoria; Sir Samuel Griffith, Premier of Queensland; John Forrest joined the ship at Albany. The voyage to England had by then been considerably shortened, thanks to the opening of the Suez Canal in 1869, so they arrived in London on 14 March, with rooms at the *Metropole* in Northumberland Avenue. The significance of this event lay in its being the first Imperial Conference, later called the British Commonwealth Prime Ministers' Conference and now – the Commonwealth Heads of Government Conference. Having attended four of these gatherings myself, as an Australian delegate in 1965, 1966, 1969 and 1971, it is easy to understand the full import of my father's status and responsibilities.

In Britain, the Conservatives were in power, led by the Marquis of Salisbury. The principal ministers concerned with Imperial Affairs, apart from the Prime Minister, were: Sir Henry Holland, the Colonial Secretary; the Earl of Onslow Under-Secretary for the Colonies; Earl Stanhope, Secretary of State; Lord George Hamilton, First Lord of the Admiralty. Neither India, the Straits Settlements, nor the Crown Colonies were represented at the Conference, since none of them were self-governing. Hence the absence of so important a minister as the Secretary of State for India. Useful, as well as pleasurable preliminaries preceded the assemblage. On 19 March, my father and his wife were presented to the Queen at Buckingham Palace. On 30 March, the Prime Minister gave a reception to the delegates. The same day the Australians met to discuss the agenda and their tactics. On 2 April, Stanhope presided at a banquet given by the Imperial Federation League for the delegates at which Downer proposed the toast of the chairman. Two days later, Salisbury opened the Conference at the Foreign Office with an eloquent speech, in which he presciently declared that though great results might not ensure immediately, this would be the parent of a long series of councils of the Empire. Holland, with whom my father already seems to have established a cordial relationship, dwelt upon the importance of defending Thursday Island and securing the independence of New Hebrides and Samoa. The delegation leaders spoke in turn. Downer departed from his usual custom by reading his speech, explaining that on account of the significance of the occasion he could not trust his emotion not to overpower his utterances. England, he said, would not regret calling the colonies to her councils.

The programme of the Conference included a diversity of subjects. Imperial defence inevitably predominated. This included defence of Australian posts, especially the Torres Straits, Table Bay and South Africa, and principal coaling stations; the election of coaling stations at various ports of the Empire; provision of harbours for the use of cruisers in the Indian Ocean; the equipment of armed cruisers in the Pacific; an increased colonial naval squadron; more facilities for using the services of Imperial officers in colonial forces. Other topics embraced relations between the colonies and foreign powers; the relations of African natives to the Empire; postal regulations between Europe and the colonies; cable communications between England and the colonies. On the legal side, the Conference sought to discuss ratification of colonial judgments by English courts other than the Privy Council, the legalisation in England of Australian marriages with a deceased wife's sister, with an attempt to achieve general agreement on legislation on this subject throughout the Empire. This was a matter on which Downer was particularly well-versed. A few days earlier, Sir Henry Holland announced in the House of Commons that special arrangements were being made for British and colonial representatives to discuss the possibilities of Imperial Federation – a subject much mooted in England at that time, but never considered practical by the colonial delegates.

The Conference sat for successive days until Maundy

Thursday 8 April, and then adjourned for a break of ten days over Easter. On that day, my father received the highest titular honour of his career by being awarded a KCMG on Salisbury's recommendation to the Queen. It must have been a happy Easter: he was only forty-two.

As is usual on these occasions, glittering hospitality abounded mainly in London but also in the provinces. On arrival, the delegates were made honorary members of the Carlton Club then, as now, a citadel of conservatism. In April they inspected the naval dockyards at Portsmouth. There was a reception at Hughenden, Disraeli's home until his death six years before. Sir Henry Holland gave a banquet attended by the Prince of Wales. The St George's Club did likewise. Lord Onslow entertained the delegates at luncheon at his beautiful country seat, *Clandon Park*. That night, my father now belonging to the order of St Michael and St George, went to a banquet at Buckingham Palace for members. Two days later, the Prince of Wales held a levee at which all the delegates were presented. At the end of the month they were feted at a banquet in the Colonial Office in the presence of the Prince of Wales who, in his speech, regretted not visiting the Cape Province and Australia – an omission he never subsequently repaired. On another occasion, Downer was given a seat in the distinguished strangers' gallery during an angry debate in the House of Commons. Another night they went to a reception at the Royal Opera House, Drury Lane.

The round of entertainments continued in May. On 4 May the Queen, now back from the south of France, received the delegates separately at Windsor. Sir John, as he now was, presented an address on behalf of South Australia, as did the leaders of all delegations for their respective countries. She then received them together, when they handed her a joint address, this being her fiftieth jubilee. That night Sir Reginald Hanson, Lord Mayor of London, held a banquet in honour of the visitors. And so it went on. The Premiers could never complain about English social largesse, a skill in which they are as adept today as nearly one hundred years ago.

The Conference, having resumed on 13 April, sat until 10 May. Compared with those that followed, this seems a long time. Did it succeed? Surely so, much more than any Commonwealth gathering in the second half of the twentieth century. The delegates agreed on a number of important topics. For the Australians, the most vital concerned naval defences of the Australian colonies. A squadron would be placed in Australian waters solely for the purpose of protecting British and colonial merchant shipping, the colonial governments contributing to its maintenance but not to exceed £120,000 a year. In return, the colonial Premiers undertook to maintain the harbours.

Albany was to be fortified with the latest modern armaments, the British agreeing to pay a larger sum towards the defence of this station. Furthermore, when discussing South Africa, it was agreed that no general scheme for the protection of Australia would be complete which did not provide ample means for the defence of Capetown. Sir Samuel Griffith's proposals for the future administration of New Guinea were accepted, the British promising to supply a cruiser. The Premiers vehemently opposed French proposals, which Salisbury floated for discussion and appeared to favour, that the New Hebrides should be ceded to France in return for which the French would send no more convicts to the Pacific. There were prolonged interchanges of views on cable lines serving Britain and Australia. The press reported Downer opposing the granting of any subsidy by the Australian colonies to any company formed to construct a Pacific cable; apparently he held that it was unnecessary and that the overland telegraph line in South Australia might suffer from the competition. As to trade, the idea for a commercial union of the Empire was examined. The delegates believed uniform tariffs to be hardly feasible, but expressed a willingness to recommend to their parliaments schemes which would favour British over foreign products. Legal problems as adumbrated in the agenda were also examined, in which Downer played a notable part.

Contemporary judgments hailed this experiment in Imperial consultation. Holland, speaking as Colonial Secretary, lauded the Conference as resulting in great permanent good to the Empire. Lord George Hamilton declared the results had ratified the partnership between Great Britain and her colonies, and would thereby aid materially in the work of welding the Empire together. The London press showed similar appreciation. the *Times* talked of 'conspicuous success'. The Adelaide *Advertiser*'s special correspondent wrote of Sir John:

> The Premier throughout the Conference has made an admirable impression. He has diligently attended to his duties, and has by every means in his power acted not only in the interest of South Australia but of Australia generally ... He may always look back with pride upon the belief but eventful visit to England upon which occasion he and his fellow representatives have taken a not ineffective step in the unity of our great Empire.

Another benefit of the Imperial conclave lay in the meeting of minds from such diverse parts of the globe, and the contacts the Premiers made with British statesmen as well as other leaders in the English community. For my father, some of these long endured. Interspersing the formal deliberations of the conference chamber with social engagements of artistic splendour enabled the delegates to mix with a variety of personalities often quite removed from politics. On all such occasions, today as much as in the past, the knowledge gained of the other men's minds is as valuable as decisions taken.

Shortly after attaining this pinnacle of achievement the Fates – for the first time in his life, though not the last – deserted him. On 14 May, Sir John and Lady Downer departed from England in the P & O *Parramatta* of 4700 tons. The voyage was uneventful until Albany. There, on 12 June, he received shattering news (in those days ships carried no wireless telegraphy). His Government lay in ruins, having fallen four days before on a non-confidence motion; his younger brother Harold; to whom he was devoted, had died. When the *Parramatta* anchored off Glenelg on 12 June, he was out of the office as well as in family mourning.

He had, of course, taken a high risk in leaving South Australia in January, parliament was expiring, and the triennial elections were due in March. The electoral system, viewed from today's standards, seems curious. Two-member constitutions are not unusual, but in a country of small population the practice of spreading a general election over five weeks could not have helped efficient public administration. The 1882 poll for the House of Assembly began on 19 March in ten metropolitan divisions; it then carried on stage by stage through the rural electorates until 20 April. Nowadays it would be unthinkable for a Premier or Prime Minister to go abroad on the eve of an election campaign, however pressing the cause. His absence undoubtedly reacted against the Ministry. Moreover, the composition of the new House differed greatly from the one he left. Only thirty-four of the fifty-two former Members returned, and of these merely thirteen had been Downer supporters. The press speculated on how the eighteen new MPs would vote. Soon after Parliament met they gave the answer. The Governor's speech enunciating the ministry's policy appears to have aroused general disappointment. There was no mention of increased tariff protection promised during the campaign. Had Sir John drafted the speech, he would have insisted on its insertion. The *Advertiser*, though tending to favour Downer, criticised the programme as being imprecise and too vague. The colony then was suffering from indifferent seasons, insufficient revenue (governments nearly a century ago were expected to live within their means), a slight economic recession and controversy over the degree of protection for local industries. Playford read the temperature of the new Assembly correctly.

On the no-confidence motion he launched, only four of the new Members voted for the Government. The outcome showed 29 for the Opposition, 16 for the Ministry, with seven abstentions. The next day, Bray as Acting-Premier placed the Ministry's resignation in the Governor's hands.

The intervening hiatus in my father's career forms a convenient place to notice the beginning of another phase of his public activities which ultimately was to bring him wider and more enduring renown than any of his accomplishments as a colonial Premier. From the early years of the Australian Colonies the idea of Federation had been mooted by occasional visionaries; the concept had appealed to my father ever since his youth. In the 1880s it crystallised into a practical beginning. A convention assembled in Sydney in 1883, with delegates from all the Australian Colonies, New Zealand, even Fiji. John downer, then Attorney-General of South Australia, attended as one of South Australia's representatives. The fruit of its deliberations was the Federal Council of Australasia, but its lack of executive and financial power, and its sporadic meetings which New South Wales, New Zealand, never attended, and Fiji only once, make it significant more as an expression of the Federal idea than as an instrument of Federation. Nevertheless, it set alight, as no previous enterprise had done, the impetus for a united nation, and some of the delegates to the 1883 meeting, were selected by their parliaments again eight years later to the much more important Sydney Convention of 1891.

Out of office, Sir John, despite his busy practice at the Bar, found more time to devote to the Federal cause. To the 1891 Convention Day each colony sent seven representatives: he was one of them. In parenthesis, it is interesting to note that New Zealand sent three delegates, but for the last time in Australia's Federal story. It was here that his friendship developed with Edmund Barton, which was to play a completely unsuspected role in his future domestic life.

We must now return to the South Australian scene. This

was a period of parliamentary instability with governments seldom enduring for more than two years. Playford having defeated Downer in 1887 was himself beaten by Cockburn in June 1889; but in August 1890 Playford turned the tables on Cockburn until FW Holder ejected him in June two years later. It was at this point that opportunity shone for my father. Early in October he carried a no-confidence motion against Holder; the Governor, the Earl of Kintore, who became his life-long friend, requested him to form an administration that was sworn in on 5 October 1892.

These were the principal portfolios in the second Downer Ministry:

| | |
|---|---|
| Premier and Chief Secretary: | Sir John Downer |
| Treasurer: | WB Rounsevell |
| Attorney-General: | R Homburg |
| Commissioner of Crown Lands: | JM Hove |
| Minister for Agriculture and Education (and Chief Secretary from May 1895): | W Conley |

Rounsevell, aged fifty, had served as Treasurer in three previous governments; his business and pastoral experience, allied with debating skill, equipped him well for these responsibilities. Homburg was a lawyer of German origin from the Barossa area, whose son and grandson over half a century later proved influential support of mine. Howe had been one of my father's Ministers in his earlier Cabinet. Copley, in the Legislative Council, enjoyed a favourable reputation as a prominent agriculturalist.

Unfortunately, this was not nearly so successful a premiership as before. The Parliament, riven by factions, lacked above all things stability. The Ministry in its short life had to be reconstructed. The general election of May 1893 weakened the Government still further. When the House met the following month, strong opposing forces marshalled behind that formidable, but not altogether admirable, character Charles Cameron

Kingston: a no-confidence motion on 16 June, deprived Sir John of his majority. Kingston, however, gave South Australia what by then it most needed – nearly six and a half years of continuous rule by combining skilfully various splinter groups. But for Downer it meant the end of his period as a minister of the Crown.

Life in opposition presented him with opportunities to advance the Federal cause as well as more time for his profession. By now his place at the bar was rivalled only by Josiah Symon, a Scot who had emigrated to Adelaide in 1865, and quickly risen to legal fame. They were destined to dislike each other, though on occasions to agree politically to become antagonists in the courts, litigants rushing to brief either one or the other. It is a moot point who was the better lawyer. My father's forensic talents with juries were unrivalled: his musical voice, his warm humanity, his understanding of the strengths and weaknesses of ordinary people, his histrionic ability – as essential in advocacy as in statecraft – placed him in a position which his many admirers considered beyond compare. His knowledge of constitutional law earned him Australia-wide respect, assisted as this was by his love of history – and a breadth of culture founded on his youthful capacity in Greek and Latin. It is his achievements in constitution-making that gave him an enduring place in Australian history.

In 1896, he suffered a severe blow. His married life had always been happy. Elizabeth gave him children, companionship, sharing warmly in his successes and reverses. Now she fell victim to cancer, and even more dreaded disease then than now. Apparently nothing could be done to arrest her condition: after much suffering she died aged only forty-nine. Momentarily shattered – for he was ever a warm, emotional, loving man – he found solace in his sons John, now twenty-four, and Fred, two years younger. Equally helpful was the support of his three surviving brothers, his sister, and their families, for all of them remained very closely knit. Perhaps even greater help came from the fascination of his work: his love of the law dominated his life. And in politics, the decisive step forward to Federation was at hand.

Early in 1897, the colonies, with the exception of Queensland, decided on an elective convention to resume the work of its 1891 predecessor. Each colony, voting as one electorate, chose ten delegates, the method being first past the post. My father won his place as a South Australian representative, and so it was that in early autumn heat, on 22 March, this famous body met for its initial deliberations in Adelaide. The setting was the Hose of Assembly chamber; fortunately for posterity the delegates were photographed outside the uncompleted Parliament buildings.

During my eight years in London as Australia's High Commissioner, it gave me pleasure to give this picture pride of place in my office at Australia House, for a more distinguished galaxy of Australians has never assembled before or since.

The next day the Convention elected Kingston president, being Premier of the host State, and Barton leader of the Convention. They then proceeded to set up three committees: Constitutional, Finance and Judiciary. Of these, the Constitution was the most important, since it had to prepare draft clauses from all three for submission to the Convention. The Constitutional Committee in turn created a Drafting Committee of three: Edmund Barton, Sir John Downer, and RE O'Conner, with RR Garran as Secretary. These men, experienced in politics and law alike, settled the form of the Australian Federation as it came into being on New Year's Day, 1901.

The Adelaide Convention sat for a month during which it completed the first draft of the Constitution. Barton stayed with my father at Pennington Terrace. Consequently, some of the work of the Drafting Committee was done in my father's study, the second room on the right of the entrance hall. This part of St Mark's College is appropriately named *The Downer House*, and a plaque by the front door commemorates the historic meetings held within. After an adjournment to discuss the draft, the Convention resumed in Sydney in September for three weeks. It was then that something happened which brought a new light into Sir John's life.

By this time, he and Barton had become close friends. They were cast in a similar mould, with shared intellectual tastes, and many interests in common, apart from the over-riding cause of Federation. The Bartons lived at *Kirribilli*, in what must have been one of Sydney's most delectable areas. Amongst their many friends were Mr and Mrs HE Russell nearby at *Keston*, a rambling Victorian house, redeemed by an attractive garden sloping down to the waterfront of Neutral Bay. Henry Russell had come to Sydney from London in 1861 as a young man on his doctor's recommendation to escape the vagaries of the English climate. Nine years later he married Frances Robey, a daughter of an early New South Wales settler, RM Robey, who had the distinction of belonging to the first Legislative Council of that colony after the grant of responsible government, from 1853 until his death in 1864. Russell, a banker and a director of several companies, had six children, three boys and three girls. The eldest, born on 9 May 1871, was Una Stella, regarded as one of the prettiest girls of her time. Artistic, well-read, adept in conversation, interested in politics (an uncle by marriage was Sir George Dibbs, a fiery Premiere of New South Wales), she was a favourite of the Bartons as well as many of the leaders of Sydney society. On a September evening in 1897, the Bartons gave a dinner party, primarily for Sir John and his eldest son whom he had brought to Sydney as a personal assistant. Una Russell was asked for young John – they were much of an age. At dinner she sat between father and son. Her partner she liked very well but the older man seemed infinitely more interesting, amusing and appealing. By the end of the evening Sir John, then fifty-three, had become vastly attracted to una, twenty-seven years his junior. Thereafter, whenever circumstances allowed, he was a frequent visitor at the Russells' house. The following year he persuaded Una to stay with him in Adelaide – suitably chaperoned, of course. On 29 November 1899 they were married in Saint John's Church, Milson's Point, with Robert Randolph Garran, the industrious Secretary of the Drafting Committee, as best man, and Muffie Barton, the Barton's eldest daughter, as one of the bridesmaids.

The final Convention meeting took place in Melbourne in February and March 1893. Sir Robert Garran, in his book *Prosper the Commonwealth*, records that the sittings opened in one of the hottest weeks known, for eight consecutive days the temperature reaching between 100 and 107.5 degrees fahrenheit. Barton and Downer stayed at the Grand, now the Hotel Windsor, diagonally opposite the Victorian Parliament where the sessions were held. The Drafting Committee met usually in Barton's hotel sitting room. Their labours were incessant, Barton himself proving the most assiduous of the three, often working into the small hours of the morning. Throughout these debates, whether in Adelaide, Sydney or Melbourne, my father fought strenuously to preserve the interest of the smaller states against the pressures of the richer and more populous New South Wales and Victoria. This applied to the proposed transfer of powers to the Commonwealth, to the authority of the Senate, hopefully designed as a States House, to financial arrangements, to the use of the River Murray waters over which he vividly appreciated South Australia's vital interests. However, burning his zeal for an Australian nation, he was fundamentally a federalist, not an unificationist. His intention lay in ceding sufficient colonial powers to the Commonwealth for it to operate on national matters common to all the states, such as defence, foreign policy, immigration, customs and exercise. He did not countenance any abdication of inherent state powers beyond what appeared necessary for Commonwealth purposes as envisaged in the 1890s. Moreover, being conservative by nature, as were the majority of his fellow delegates, he and his colleagues deliberately made the Constitution difficult to alter – not selfishly to imprison it within the ideas of their day, but to safeguard the compact, to prevent sudden rushes of public opinion, which from time to time erupt in all democracies, from overturning the considered opinions and compromises of years of thought and discussion by a vote reflecting the passions of the moment rather than a carefully deliberated view. Hence the restrictive provisions for constitutional alteration, so frustrating to subsequent generations of governments and against which many of us have recoiled as being too rigid to cope with the revolutionary charges of the twentieth century. Yet, on balance, were the authors of the Constitution wrong in the light of subsequent political history? Did they not, in fact, exhibit a perspicacity lacking in contemporary political protagonists? They certainly have prevented Australia from becoming a socialist or communist state. They have made it extremely difficult for radical politicians to ditch the monarchy. They have ensured a division of powers in a country diverse in its problems, its attitudes, whose territorial dimension is similar to Europe or the United States. No human institution, of course, should remain static, and nearly eight years experience has shown the need for some degree of constitutional amendment. I subscribe to some myself. But the basic concept of our constitutions should be preserved at least until such time as the Australian people as a result of protracted meditation and deliberation determine whether they wish for a different system of government. Meanwhile, for what we have received from the founding fathers we should be profoundly grateful.

On 17 March the Convention completed its labours, with especial eulogies for the work of the Drafting committee. The delegates speedily returned to their respective communities to secure endorsement for the Constitution by referendum. Sir John and his colleagues conducted a state-wide campaign, with meetings surprisingly poorly attended. At Gawler, for example, the principal town of his Barossa electorate, he mustered merely one hundred people. Voting took place on 3 June in

New South Wales, Victoria, South Australia and Tasmania. Western Australia deferred her decision; Queensland, unrepresented at the Second Convention, looked on from the ring-side uncertain at this point whether she should join the Federation at all. Victoria, South Australia, and Tasmania produced overwhelming affirmatives – Victoria 100,580 to 22,000; South Australia 35,390 to 17,320; Tasmania 11,797 to 2716. Regrettably, New South Wales failed to reach her previously agreed 'Yes' quota of 80,000, the figures being 71,595 for the Constitution and 65,288 against. This meant the case had to be argued all over again. A Premiers' Conference in Melbourne – fortunately attended by Queensland – agreed to subject to their parliaments seven amendments to the Constitution. These were accepted, and a new referendum was held in South Australia – later in other States – on 29 April, 1899. The result everywhere was conclusive, with a much larger poll in each of the four participants of the year before. South Australia now opted 65,900 to 17,953 against. When Western Australia, in 1900, came in with more than a two to one majority for Federation, the battle, except for difficulties with the British Government mainly over Privy Council appeal, had been won.

What is curious, looking back after seventy-five years, is the apathy of the Australian public to the whole Federal cause. South Australia was typical of the other colonies. In the first referendum only 53,120 people voted out of 152,000 enrolled; in 1899, the score showed more enthusiasm but still merely 55 per cent of the electorate. Compulsory voting in those days was unknown; not until 1925 did the Bruce Government introduce it for Federal elections. The Boer War had broken out in 1899, evoking voluntary military contingents from each of the colonies in support of what they regarded as the 'Mother Country', and naturally this was a first call on pubic attention. But search as one does for explanations, it is one of the strange and rather discreditable ironies of Australian democracy: that when it came to the culmination of the struggle for an Australian nation after twenty years exposition and controversy by some of the finest minds our country had yet produced, a little more than half of those entitled took the trouble to express an opinion at the ballot box. The Imperial Parliament passed the Commonwealth of Australia Constitution Bill early in the northern summer of 1900, Queen Victoria assenting to it on 9 July. In the King's Hall of Parliament House, Canberra, thousands of visitors every year gaze at the table, and the pen, used by the old Queen for this purpose, then in the last year of her life. New Year's Day 1901 was proclaimed the date for the Australian Commonwealth to come into being; elections for the first Senate and House of Representatives were fixed for 30 March 1901. The Constitution provided for six Senators from each of the six States, and a House of Representatives of seventy-five members. Not surprisingly, most of the Federal leaders felt attracted by the new National Parliament, and offered themselves accordingly.

Sir John preferred the Senate to the lower House, I think because from the vantage point of what was intended to be the States House he believed he could better safeguard State interests. This involved severing his connection with the Barossa division which he had represented with unbroken continuity for close on twenty-three years. His constituents presented him with a splendidly bound illuminated address, elaborately decorated in *fin de siecle* taste, amidst many encomiums and expressions of regret at the Gawler Town Hall. At the elections, with the whole State voting as one constituency, he came fourth out of the first six, a surprising result for one who all along had occupied such a prominent place in the Federal movement, and had contributed so richly to the form of the Constitution. The other South Australian Senators were his old friend Sir Richard Baker, his frequent antagonist in the courts Sir Josiah Symon, Thomas Playford (who earlier had declined a knighthood), DM Charleston, and G McGregor, the last two belonging to the Labor Party, then in its infancy.

The first Commonwealth Parliament met in Melbourne. To satisfy New South Wales opinion, it had previously been agreed that the Federal capital should be in the State but not less that one hundred miles from Sydney; until the site was chosen, the temporary capital should be Melbourne. So to Melbourne, amidst great panoply, came the Duke and Duchess of York, later George V and Queen Mary, to open Parliament in the Exhibition Building. The date was 9 May, my mother's thirtieth birthday. This historic event is commemorated by a fine picture now hanging in the Exhibition Building, showing a becoming portrait of my father standing at the beginning of the third row of members. The better known impression of Tom Roberts is too crowded to interpret the occasion as it must have seemed.

For the next twenty-six years Melbourne remained Australia's seat of government. Both houses met in the handsome neo-classic Victorian Parliament, little changed to this day. My mother used to accompany my father for the sittings; they stayed at what is now the Hotel Windsor, and remained there for long periods of the session. Apart from the political fascination of these opening years of Federation, hospitality often on the elaborate scale characterised Melbourne life. This naturally appealed to a young woman such as my mother whose zest for parties equalled her interest in art, religion and politics. Their experiences were varied and plentiful. One night, driving in a carriage with Sir William and Lady M'Millan to a dinner at Federal Government House, the horses shied at the intersection between Young and Jackson's Hotel and Flinders Street Railway Station. The coachman lost control, a collision ensured, both my father and M'Millan received cuts in the face, the ladies were badly bruised and shaken. In fact, all were lucky to escape far worse injury. Bedraggled and late, they somehow managed to arrive, to the astonishment and sympathy of their hosts and fellow guests.

The government House parties were many and glamorous, with not only the Governor-General but the State Governor in town. The youthful Lord Hopetoun was the first, though not very successful, Governor-General. His action shortly after his arrival at the end of 1900, in asking Sir William Lyne instead of Edmund Barton to form a government which, of course, the distrusted Lyne was unable to do, was an irrecoverable blunder. Two years later he was succeeded by the highly respected Governor of South Australia, Lord Tennyson, the poet's son. The Tennysons were friends of my parents and were as hospitable to the young as to the more successful. My mother used to tell the story how, after one of their Government House balls, the swans in the lake were suffering from obstructions in their throats. Careful examination revealed they had swallowed contraceptives. The Edwardian decade had already begun.

The debates of the first Federal Parliament 1901-1903 are amongst the most important in the story of the Australian Commonwealth. For it was during these sessions that foundations of national policy were laid which were to last for decades, and some of which still endure. My father, then aged fifty-six to fifty-nine, was at the height of his powers. His mature thinking on the Constitution, the British Empire, the High Court, the protection versus free trade controversy, customs tariffs, the national capital, immigration policy, the role of the Senate, proportional representation, women's suffrage, are succinctly expressed in his speeches recorded in Hansard. Particularly notable is the first of these delivered on 23 May 1901 in the *Address-in-Reply* debate. Left-wing writers fifty years later portrayed him as an arch-conservative; if they had researched his record and his speeches they would have discovered his advocacy of some measures dear to the heart of modern radical politicians such as Mr Whitlam. Thus we find him saying in 1901 that railways should be under Federal control. Rather reluctantly, he voted for the *Immigration Bill* which proclaimed the White Australia policy, and introduced the dictation (then called the education) test. He could see no urgency for this legislation; he did not believe large numbers of Indians and Asians would wish to settle in Australia; he denounced as selfishness refusal to permit coloured people admission to Northern Australia if climatic difficulties precluded British and Europeans from developing those tropical regions. He recalled his attitude a few years earlier, saying he was probably wrong, but it seems to express his innermost feeling:

> I strongly opposed legislation of this kind in the South Australian Parliament. I thought it was unnecessary; and I entertained a general notion – something like that held by Mr Chamberlain about the English traditions – that Britishers generally consider themselves strong enough to hold their own. It was a wrong opinion, no doubt, but the feeling I had was that if a better man could meet me on my own ground I did not care much what his colour was, I thought he was entitled to win.

That argument, he continued, was fallacious because of the instinct of self-preservation. Nonetheless, it indicated where his sentiments lay. Nor did he want to embarrass the British Government by legislation which not only Indian, African, and Caribbean members of the Empire would find discriminatory, but also the Japanese with whom Britain recently had concluded a treaty. But because of strong pubic opinion on this issue, and of undertakings given in the election campaign, he considered, despite his own hesitations, that Senators were obliged to support the Ministry's proposals.

His views on appeals from Australian courts to the Privy Council were similarly in advance of majority opinion at the turn of the century. These are expounded at length both in his *Address-and-Reply* speech and to years later on the Judiciary bill. As far back as the first Federal Convention in 1891 he had contended that the High Court should act as the ultimate court of appeal in the land. He regretted the compromise made in 1900 at the behest of Mr Chamberlain, the British colonial Secretary, motivated, he believed, 'by an exceedingly active minority from the States.' Thus:

> In the Convention of 1891 … we agreed on a clause which prevented appeals to the Privy Council except in cases in which the imperial Government considered that their position with other countries was involved … The Convention of 1891 thought that we were quite competent to manage our own judicial affairs amongst ourselves. That opinion I vehemently contended for at the time. That opinion I have never moved from up to the present moment … The primary idea we had was to be our own ultimate judges and not to have appeals out of the Commonwealth except in matters which might involve the Old Country in trouble with other people (*Address-in-Reply*, 1901).

He spelt this out more fully and more critically in his speech on the Judiciary Bill on 5 August 1903:

> We were of the opinion (in the 1897 Convention) that there was no necessity for appeal to a foreign tribunal which knew not our wants, which knew not the reasons for our legislation, which was absolutely unacquainted with our surroundings, and which so far as we were concerned conducted its deliberations in the dark, so that we were ignorant of its proceedings until a decision was given. The Privy Council consists of a number of eminent men and a number of men of less eminence. It is a tribunal very varied in its assortment, and a magnificent tribunal if the Bench which is called together happens to be composed of the best. It is not such a good tribunal, however, if the best of the members do not happen to attend: at all events, it is a tribunal which, from its constitution, requires none of the most excellent to attend, but which is composed of stray gentlemen, sometimes more able, sometimes less able … The Privy Council decide on our intentions and our circumstances with which we ourselves ought to be acquainted, and have to be guided by the evidence of experts when we here would require no such assistance.

Sir John considered the establishment of the High court to be a matter of cardinal importance – and urgency.

> I look upon the judiciary as the very basement of the Constitution. Without it the Constitution simply cannot

> work; without it the Constitution would never have been proposed, and without it the Constitution would never have been accepted by the people.

Parliament should provide for a very powerful court. He regretted the House of Representatives reducing the number of judges – five – originally proposed, to three.

> I look upon the question of expense, which has been made so much of, as being simply beneath contempt … The Constitution cannot work satisfactorily unless the High Court is competent, and undoubtedly it needs not merely the weight of intellect but the weight of numbers as well in order to prevent the ill-feeling which comes from appealing from a larger number of judges to a smaller number.

In the same speech he made some observations which governments of the future should always need:

> The Constitution is in a way rigid; it is elastic in substance. The judges to administer this Constitution ought to be much more than lawyers. They ought to be great constitutional lawyers from the Federal point of view. Look at the ambit of the subject – matters of our jurisdiction; look at our thirty-five articles, and see what they cover.

He enumerated some of them, pointing out they were borrowed from the United States constitution, and continued:

> Trade and commerce is an exceedingly extensive term. The words are rigid enough, their meaning is elastic enough in all conscience, and they have been treated by the great Chief Justice Marshall (in America) and others in a manner which has considerably expanded them in accordance with the spirit of the Constitution, and in a way which has proved beneficial entirely to the community. We have come to see the immense wisdom of using these terse words which, though precise, were yet capable of infinite expansion to meet the development of the republic as time went on … The development of the American republic is a marvellous justification of the use of terse language, but at the same time we must have competent exponents of it, and further, it must be interpreted according to the spirit of the

> times, and for that purpose we must have people who are sympathetic with the spirit of the time, who know what is going on, and who will accurately interpret the law so as to meet the demands which an altered set of circumstances require.

These are the words of a statesman of profound perception. Regrettably, despite the rare quality of various High Court judges, Cabinets over a period of nearly eighty years have not always appointed men who satisfied these criteria.

At the time of Federation, the main political controversy was not private enterprise versus socialism but between protection and free trade. In this respect my father was a pragmatist, with protectionist leanings, as his Premiership of South Australia shows. He summarised his position in his speech on the *Address-in-Reply*:

> They asked me at home … if I was a free trader, and I said no; they said are you a protectionist and I said no. They said are you sitting on a rail, and I said yes, a very hight rail, too, from which I can get the perspective of what is going on, and can come down on this side and do the best for my fellows, and then down on the other side, and do what is best and going up again, and not be grovelling in the dirt with a lot of beetles of men who cannot see an inch in front of their noses. I say all this talk about free trade and protection is pure rubbish. We cannot find a true free-trader anywhere anymore than we can find a true protectionist; they are all opportunists as they ought to be … I say a plague on both; there is no truth in either. We have to do the best we can in the circumstances.

In the 1880s he must have felt circumstances in South Australia demanded protection, because as he told the Senate during the debate on the Customs Tariff Bill 1902, he had introduced the first protective tariff in the South Australian Parliament.

He had very firm views on the Constitution and on the place of the Senate in it. Repeatedly in debates came the phrase, 'I base myself on the Constitution.' Speaking on the *Address-in-Reply* he declared:

> We practically founded our Constitution on the basis of the American as far as it could be so founded with a Constitution under the Crown ... The basis of the American Constitution and ours is that the Senate shall be a body at least co-ordinate in authority with the House of Representatives ... As far as we could, the struggle of myself and a good many more who were working on the same side, was to establish a constitution on the basis so firm that its identity would not be lost in any sudden wave of popular feeling that might sweep over the Continent of Australia, and to establish it on a basis so sound and firm that ultimately the people's will rule as it always must, but still so that every possible safeguard should be interposed to guarantee that it was the popular will that was being expressed, and not the ephemeral excitement of the moment. We did not get all we wanted but we got a good deal, and whether we get all we want depends upon the manner in which this House uses the power given to it; the extent to which it proves itself worthy of the authority given to it, and proves itself equal to the responsibility of accepting the opprobrium which may at times fall upon it through taking up a proper constitutional position.

The Senate, he maintained, was not a Legislative Council but a body representing the individual States – a State House apart from the people's house, and going to the very root of the Constitution which is that the States must agree as well as the people in the States before legislation is determined upon.

Later he continued:

> We cannot introduce Money bills, and although ... we cannot amend them, yet a power equal to that is given to us in the form of suggestion. So that, as a matter of fact, we can amend them in effect, and if the result is that our amendments are not agreed to ... on the House which refuses the amendments rests the ultimate responsibility of the ultimate rejection of these measures rather than the House that proposed the amendments. At all events we

> have the power; but whether we can exercise the power will depend … on the personnel of the first Senate of the Commonwealth of Australia.

Finally – and here he made a prediction which rapidly became falsified – 'I have a feeling … we will hold our own in the great constitutional position, and not allow our House to be subordinated to any party considerations.' By the end of the decade, party considerations were moulding the Senate's decisions; by 1920, it had deteriorated unblushingly into a Party House. By the middle of the century it had departed so far from the intentions of the framers of the Constitution as to be neither the House of the States (except in its form of election) nor a body, by and large, of conspicuous quality.

Sir John's views on women's suffrage were also in advance of those generally held. Ever since a young man he advocated votes for women. These he reiterated in the Senate debate on the Franchise Bill in April 1902. At that time, South Australia and Western Australia were the only States with female enrolment. Not until 1918 did women get the vote in Britain, a process only completed in 1923 when the Baldwin administration extended full voting rights to women aged twenty-one. Although from his South Australian experience he considered that women voted much the same as men – especially those who were married – he always possessed an exalted conception of them. Thus his declaration in the same debate:

> I think that women are better than men, and have purer and higher notions, but I am sure they are very much open to the influence of those who have not notions so high or so noble as their own.

But whilst agreeing with the Barton Government's legislation for a uniform adult franchise throughout Australia, he did not favour 'at present' women becoming members of the Federal Parliament. Had he lived longer, perhaps he would have changed his mind.

Some of his ideas were not subsequently accepted. He did not like single-member electorates. No doubt flowing from his South Australian experiences of two-member constituencies, he considered the latter provided a better opportunity for representation of minorities. Nor did he approve of electing the Senate by proportional representation. In a long, lively and trenchant speech on the Electoral Bill in February 4902, he strongly opposed this measure, believing it violated the spirit of the Constitution. For the Federal capital he favoured Bombala, distrusting the possibility – this was before the age of commercial aircraft – of a New South Wales government impeding the free access to a territory which was an enclave of that State. And – although the question did not arise in the first Commonwealth Parliament, and though possessing no inherited wealth of his own – he never supported payment of large salaries to MPs. When the Government in 1906 increased the meagre £400 a year to £600, he roundly denounced this from a public platform. In Imperial affairs he allied himself with British Conservatives who opposed Home Rule for Ireland, fearing that such a move would mark the first stage in the disintegration of the United Kingdom. Socialism, both in doctrine and in application, was anathema.

With the launching of the Commonwealth, Sir John suffered one of his major disappointments. He may not have expected a portfolio in the first ministry. There were only nine places: Barton, universally admired and acknowledged as principal Federal leader, commanded an unrivalled claim for the Prime Ministership, as the unwise Hopetoun soon realised. The State Premiers, too, enjoyed a precedence which could not be overlooked. Thus Sir John Forrest from Western Australia, Sir Philip Fysh from Tasmania, Sir George Turner from Victoria entered the Cabinet. So did Lyne, the Premier of New South Wales, despite his inability to form a government of his own. Kingston who the previous year had been ejected from office after six and a half years as Premier of South Australia, and despite his personal faults, was an astute politician and a prominent federalist, represented South Australia. Sir Robert Philip, the Queensland Premier, declined; in his stead Barton chose Sir James Dickson, the previous Premier, and after his death Senator JG Drake. State representation in Federal cabinet-making, then as now, precludes many a superior man form an office he could adorn. The two remaining portfolios went to New South Wales and Victoria: RE O'Connor (of the Drafting Committee) and the oratorical Alfred Deakin.

My father, coming from one of the smaller States, with his long political experience and realism, appreciated the practical limitations on Barton's preferences. Nevertheless a position which would have been much to his liking had been suggested. The Constitution provided for a High Court of Australia as the nation's supreme tribunal; it was charged with the ever more decisive function of interpreting the Constitution as an arbiter between the States, and between the States and the Commonwealth. Originally in the 1902 Bill, five judges were proposed, one of whom was to be Downer. But when the revised legislation came before Parliament in 1903, the proposed Court had shrunk to three. By that time Barton was suffering from overwork; his doctors told him to lighten his duties. On 23 September he resigned as Prime Minister, becoming one of the High Court judges. The same evening O'Connor retired from the Government, taking the third place on the Bench. Magnanimously, Barton offered the Chief Justiceship to Samuel Griffith, Australia's most distinguished jurist of the day, who was not only Chief Justice of Queensland but the principal author of the 1801 draft constitution. Thus two of the three members – and close friends – of the Drafting Committee were requited first with ministerial, then with judicial, office. For Sir John there was nothing, except a broken promise.

The sequel to this incident was perhaps inevitable. My father felt he had been let down by his friends; some years elapsed before he and Barton became reconciled. And of course, the three judges soon found the work insurmountable. In 1906 the Deakin Cabinet appointed two more. Two of the more radical members of the 1897–98 Convention were chosen, both Victorians: Isaacs and Higgins. The twist they deliberately have to the Constitution marked the beginning of the conflicts within the High Court, and deepened the suspicions the States already were harbouring towards the Commonwealth.

The first National Parliament ended prematurely in November 1903. Deakin had succeeded Barton as Prime Minister: no doubt he desired his own mandate. Having seen the Federation launched, my father felt no urge to continue. He was not well-off financially, being dependent entirely on his earnings at the Bar, and whatever savings he could effect. Politics, he used to say, kept him a poor man. Federal members initially received £400 a year, in purchasing power no more than £4000 today. Moreover, with Parliament sitting in Melbourne it was impossible to maintain his legal practice to anything like the same degree as when he belonged to the South Australian Assembly. He therefore declined to stand for re-election, and so by 1904, after nearly twenty-six years of parliamentary service, he found himself out of politics.

But not for long. The following year a vacancy occurred in the Legislative Council for the Southern district. This covered an extensive part of the State, from the Mount Lofty Ranges right down to Mount Gambier and the Victorian border. Being asked to stand, he willingly did so. Though not particularly onerous, his membership of the Council restored him to political life which he loved so well; at the same time it enabled him to continue his work at the Bar, where he flourished during the ensuing years in a series of leading cases.

The South Australian Legislative Council is a body which throughout its history had undergone variations in size. During Sir John's ten years it contained eighteen members, elected on a slightly restrictive franchise, from four multiple constituencies. I do not think he was ever interested in holding office in this last lap of his career. Sixty-one when elected, he preferred the role of elder statesman which he played with resounding effect. It is no exaggeration to say he dominated the chamber; indeed one observer wrote that South Australia at that time had two Houses: a Lower House and a Downer House.

In 1910, an unexpected domestic event occurred which gave him particular pleasure and pride. Although he and my mother had been married since the end of 1899, there were no children. By 1906 he grew reconciled to this, believing, as he wrote to a friend, that if Una did have a child, he would never live to see it grown up. Fate decided otherwise. On 7 April 1910 his fourth son was born, and christened by the Bishop of Adelaide a few weeks later – Alexander Russell. Not every man of sixty-five can display the same genetic prowess.

In December 1910, my father and mother, taking their baby and a nurse, left the Orient liner *Otranto* for a year abroad. Edward VII had died in May; his son George V and Queen Mary were to be crowned on 22 June 1911. My parents were invited to the coronation, and they took the opportunity of spending the remaining part of the European winter in Italy, where they had a private audience of Pope Pius X, Switzerland, the Riviera, and Paris. Arriving in London in spring, they at first took a flat in Queen Anne's Gate, bordering St James' Park; towards the end of their stay, after visiting friends and sightseeing in the country, they moved to St Ermins, Westminster. The year provided one of those long, hot English summers that come to be celebrated in song and story. This was fortunate for my mother on the first of her several long stays in England. For my father, apart from the splendours of the coronation, his return to England after an absence of twenty-four years enabled him to meet not only surviving associates of the first Imperial Conference, former Governors and Governor-Generals, but many of the lending statesmen of the day. He was frequently asked to speak at banquets in the London season, on one occasion through no fault of his own, colliding with

Lord Carrington, a Liberal senior cabinet minister, at a Royal Colonial Institute dinner over which Carrington presided. Sir John was so affronted by Carrington's rudeness that, in the most dignified manner possible, he declined to proceed with his speech. Controversy ensued in the press, with headlines in the conservative newspapers such as, 'Dominion Statesman Insulted'. Many people wrote to him in the most sympathetic way, especially those antagonistic to Asquith's Liberal Government. Politically, the air was explosive. There had been two general elections in 1910 caused first by George Lloyd's radical budget the year before, and ensuing dissension between the House of Commons and House of Lords leading to the restrictions placed on the latter by the 1911 Parliament Act. Lord Carrington's touchiness, when my father began to praise the usefulness of the referendum as a constitutional device, is understandable, but for a Minister of Carrington's experience, his behaviour brought him no credit. As my father never retained animosities, he would probably smile benignly today on the fact that Carrington's great-nephew, the present Lord Carrington, has long been one of my most warmly regarded friends.

My mother used to say that all the high peaks of her life were marred by clouds. After her engagement to my father, her mother, with whom she shared a great devotion, suddenly died. After her marriage, happy in every way, she contracted heart disease, and for two or three years had to lead a restricted life. At the end of this brilliant season in London, they received shattering news that my father's eldest son, John, had died before his thirty-ninth birthday. They sought quiet and solace in Devon, but especially for my father, sorrow darkened the rest of the year. In November they sailed for home in the *Orama* on her maiden voyage, arriving in Adelaide in time for Christmas at *Glenalta*.

I am often asked if I remember my father, yes I do vividly, albeit with the picture postcard memory of a child. Essentially a generous, affectionate man, with a deep love of his family, he entertained strong opinions which occasionally bordered on intolerance. In his dealings, both professional and political, he was forthright, and honourable to a degree exceeded by none of his associates. Although ambitious, he was devoid of ruthlessness: had he shown less consideration for others he might have attained higher success. Loyalty to his friends was one of his hallmarks. He helped Sir Richard Baker, at sacrifice to himself, to secure sufficient support for election to the office of first President of the Senate. For others he appeared sometimes to stand aside, to his own disadvantage. I suspect that had he pressed his just claims for preferment with the artifices of many lesser politicians, his place would have been higher in the first Commonwealth Parliament.

Both as a public speaker and a parliamentary debater he stood in the front rank. Lady Tennyson once told my mother that she would hear no better speaker in England than Sir John. He combines serious argument with wit, trenchant denunciation with homely illustration springing from his innate understanding of ordinary men and women. In criminal cases in the courts he at times moved juries to tears in defence of his client; he was equally successful with judges over difficult points of equity and common law. In all this his well modulated, cultured voice, his capacity for epigram, for original phrase, enriched his reputation. And his classical education gave him a comprehension of our language denied to most of those without this benefit.

In his earlier years of public life some people found him too decided in his views. A commentator in the early 1880s complained of him being rather imperious. Deakin writing of his fellow delegates to the 1897–98 Convention, described Sir John as more mellow than in the assemblage of 1891. If he was stung by an opponent his immediate reaction could be brusque. Sir Angas Parsons, the senior puisne judge of the south Australian Supreme Court in the 1930s and 1940s, related to me how once when he had acted as junior counsel on the opposite side, my father had turned on him with withering aggression. The next time they met, Parsons mildly remonstrated Sir John, he said, dissolved him with a smile, saying 'My dear fellow, I'm really very sorry.'

As a political tactician he was adroit, but I suspect too intellectually honest to be a great general in the House. In the 1890s, when he secured his second term as Premier, he lacked the cunning of Kingston – whom he disliked and distrusted – to combine discordant elements. Sometimes he was criticised in his later years for indolence; people who were well-wishers thought he could have made more of his brilliance, and of his opportunities. Yet here is a judgment of one of his contemporaries. Sir John Cockburn, writing to Simpson Newland in 1920, said:

> I often think of our old association in the Ministry. Now that Jim Howe has gone there are, I think, only you and I left of the old Downer Government ... Of all the leasers I have been associated with, John Downer stands out as a chivalrous, honourable and straight-forward man.

His wide vision extended to many subjects. Possessing profound faith in what Australia could become, in the Melbourne Town Hall in 1909, and again at a St George's day dinner in Adelaide in 1913, he warned that to the north of us lay ancient, thickly populated civilisations, that we would forfeit our right to hold this continent if we lacked a determination to develop and populate it. Australia's population at that time numbered merely four million; we should, he said, be thinking of twelve million not four. Privately, despite his love of England and his veneration of many things British, he foreshadowed their social and industrial upheavals that lay ahead. Social changes throughout Britain would be more pronounced, more disturbing for the propertied classes, than any which might eventuate in Australia. Again, though no man showed loftier local patriotism or more gratitude to his community, he affirmed his primary allegiance to Australia as a nation rather than his own State.

He had, of course, other interests besides law and politics. After his retirement from the Senate, he joined the Adelaide University Council. Later, he became president of the Commonwealth Club, a luncheon body which provides for visiting speakers as good a cross-section of the community as exists in Australia. A voracious reader, he captivated his family and friends by interpretations from his favourite works. Almost inevitably, being himself a product of the nineteenth century, he revelled in authors of that period: beautifully bound editions of Scott, Thackeray, Dickens, Bronte, Kingsley projected prominently in his library. He could quote page after page of Dickens with an accuracy astonishing to his listeners. Shakespeare he loved; he had a taste for poetry from Wilton to Tennyson. In an intellectual sense, religion played a high part in his life. Well-versed in the scriptures, he possessed an advantage in being able to read some of the texts in the original Greek. Religious problems and controversies, so characteristic of the Victorian age, interested him. These he followed closely as is apparent from his bookshelves. In the broad sense he was a believer: perhaps not quite sure of the life of the world to come – but hopeful. He described himself as a buttress of the Church of England from outside rather than within. He developed a friendship with two of Adelaide's most notable bishops, Harmer and Kennion, regretting deeply the latter's translation to Bath and Wells. But he never confined his ecclesiastical friendship to his own faith: throughout his career he demonstrated a sympathetic disposition towards the Roman Church, which was cordially reciprocated, whilst one of the principal friends of his later life, the great preacher Henry Howard (who in the 1920s became pastor of the Fifth Avenue Presbyterian Church in New York) was the leading Methodist minister of South Australia. The moving memoir Howard wrote after my father's death is probably the best index of his spiritual attitudes.

My father attracted many friends, and he enjoyed social life. He mixed easily with all classes, possessed a keen sense of humour, was a remarkable raconteur, a generous host who appreciated good food and fine wines, occasionally as with many of his generation, to excess. A cigar was never far away; in fact, cigars, though not through any affectation, became part of his stock-in-trade as with Churchill, and Harold Wilson with his pipe. Apart from the ever-increasing members of the Downer family, and his close political and intellectual ties with men such as Barton, O'Connor, Forrest and Baker, he had long shared a firm friendship with personalities as diverse as Henry Dutton, the squire of Anlaby, James Martin on whose engineering works at Gawler rested that town's economy, Sir Samuel Way, South Australia's Chief Justice since 1876, and many members of the legal profession. He saw much of Mr and Mrs Robert Barr Smith, being a frequent guest at their elegant, sumptuous parties whether at *Torrens Park* (now Scotch College), their house in Angas Street, or their country house *Auchindarroch*, Mount Barker. Indeed, Joanna Barr Smith, herself one of South Australia's most gracious women, was an especially dear friend, as her many benefactions to my parents bear witness. My mother described her as the most remarkable woman she had ever met.

The best photographic likeness of Sir John is at the opening of the 1897 Convention; of medium height, his broad shoulders give him a sturdy appearance. His brown hair never turned completely grey, and it thinned only slightly towards the end of his life. Always well-covered, he inclined to fat as he grew older, in his last years too much so. In repose his face, always clean-shaven, seemed determined, strong, and stern, but a twinkle was never far away from those clear grey-blue eyes often looking into a distance he was ever trying to perceive. If at first he appeared to be a trifle forbidding, the impression instantly dissolved by a smile of warmth and charm of which no one ever forgot. He was meticulous in his dress: the fashion, compared with the present, demanded formality from men of position. Nor was he in any sense an athlete or sporty person like his two elder brothers or his nephews. As a young man he rode a lot – there were scarcely any options – and to the last he retained his skill with horses. He delighted in walking, which he did whenever he could between Pennington Terrace and his office, and as a small boy I remember his telling me of the wisdom of regular exercise. At *Glenalta* he enjoyed painting gates, fences, bridge railings across the creek, donning a white suit for this purpose. Despite his great intellect, and his liking for fine living, he was at heart a simple man who loved being at home with his family, friends, and books. Perhaps this explains, in part, his lack of vanity, which is so often found amongst politicians.

The remaining years of my father's life marked the end of an epoch in the world history. He had long felt apprehensive about Germany's designs, sadly the culminating act of the tragedy of 1914 came as no surprise to him. But other shadows were gathering too. That year he started to decline physically from recurrent bouts of ill-health. Early in 1915 more disturbing symptoms of digestive disorder appeared. As the year progressed he knew he was afflicted by cancer. The doctors operated to provide some temporary relief, but eventually his system was incapable of receiving nourishment. About three o'clock in the morning of 2 August, whilst my mother was sitting by his bed, he suddenly clasped her with both arms in an embrace which left her breathless, then turned over and died.

There are memorials to him in Canberra, where a suburb is named after him, and the Downer Fountain in Garema Place. In Adelaide, his town house where he lived and died, now part of St Mark's College, is called the 'Downer House'. In a courtyard at the rear, a bronze fountain of St Mark stands in his honour. At St Peter's College, the John William Downer scholarship recalls his schooldays there. In the Northern Territory, a range of hills commemorates him. By the front of Parliament House, Adelaide, a plaque records the work of the Drafting

Committee, and inside his name appears on the honour roll of Premiers of South Australia. But his real memorial consists neither in these embellishments nor in his descendants who deeply revere him: his name is enshrined in Australia's history, and his shadow lengthens with the passage of the years.

## *Chapter 8*

# Harold Field Downer 1847–1887

This is a story of genius cut off in its prime. The youngest of Henry and Jane Downer's children, he was born in Adelaide on 5 November 1847. If an astrologer had been able to cast his horoscope correctly, the predictions would have foretold a short, brilliant, varied, somewhat unconventional life in two hemispheres.

At first he went to Mr Haire's school, afterwards to St Peter's where he carried off many academic distinctions. He was said to have proved himself probably the first scholar of his time. Like his brother John, he displayed a remarkable aptitude for the classics; unlike John he shone as a mathematician. There being no university in Adelaide, his brother George provided the means of his going to Cambridge, towards the close of the 1860s. It was here, in common with many young man before and since, that he engaged in other pursuits besides learning.

From Cambridge, Harold proceeded to Paris, working as a lecturer in English either at the Sorbonne or some other educational institution. In the early 1870s, he forsook the fascinations of Europe for Adelaide, and after re-adjusting himself to a colonial environment decided to follow three of his brothers into the legal profession. For this his mind seem particularly suited; he became articled to George, and so learnt the practical as well as the theoretical side of the law in the offices of G & J Downer. In 1876 he was called to the Bar. After Henry Downer's decision to embark on politics, involving his resignation as Commissioner of Insolvency in 1881, Henry and Harold joined forces under the caption of HE & HF Downer. The stage was now set for a meteoric rise which, had he been more fortunate in health, could have led him to the highest pinnacles of his profession.

He quickly attracted the admiration of judges and practitioners alike. In a complex, difficult case, Laffan versus Graves, chief Justice Way declared that 'Mr Downer's argument for the plaintiff was unsurpassed in force in the annals of the South Australian Bar.' Clients and colleagues found him industrious almost to a fault. His temperament was more inclined to logical, measured, argument characteristic of appeal cases rather than the dramatic eloquence of an advocate before a jury. Contemporaries praised his courteous manner, responding to a quiet calm emanating from a lovable disposition. Some people at first found him reserved, almost retiring; to others his exterior appeared always calm, on occasion slightly cynical, disguising an exceptional intellect beneath the surface. Possibly he lacked the humour as a speaker for which Sir John was so noted. Generous in temperament, he hated unfairness and oppression. As a commentator wrote, once seized of the idea that a client was a victim or likely to become such of either of these forces, he would do everything in his power to see that justice was done.

Harold's principal misfortune lay in lacking the physical robustness of his brothers. When only thirty-six, he showed warning signs of consumption. To receive the best advice available, he left for England early in 1885 to consult Sir Andrew Clarke, one of London's leading physicians. Clark urged him to recuperate in the Alps. So he went to Switzerland where, being of an adventurous nature and fond of mountaineering, he attempted the ascent of Mont Blanc. In this he took a grave risk, for summer was not sufficiently advanced. As ill-luck would have it, he and his companions encountered extreme cold; one of his legs was so badly frostbitten that he had to take refuge in a mountain chalet until he could move freely. After further vicissitudes in which all plans of continuing the expedition were abandoned, Harold returned to London in very poor shape. For weeks he was confined to his room. Eventually he sailed for Adelaide, arriving at the beginning of 1886. Far from his sojourn in England and the Continent benefiting him, his physical plight looked worse than when he departed the previous year. However, shortly afterwards he left for a few weeks in Melbourne, as a result of which he felt sufficiently well to resume his practice in Adelaide. The remainder of 1886 saw him involved in several important cases in which, as was his nature, he did not spare himself. But by January 1887, his condition alarmed his friends to such an extent that try as he would he could only work intermittently. By now nothing was able to arrest his decline, and early in the morning of Monday 23 May, he died in the house of his sister Amelia on North Terrace aged thirty-nine.

The place of Harold Downer in the South Australian community can be gauged by public reaction at the news of his death. The *Advertiser* on 24 May published three articles about him: a long obituary notice, a leader and a personal sketch. The *Register* on the same day wrote a lengthy obituary, and a leading article. Some excerpts are worth quoting to illustrate the esteem this comparatively young man had aroused amongst his contemporaries. 'By the death of Mr Harold Downer', said the *Register*,

> the legal profession had lost one of its brightest ornaments, and South Australia one of her most estimable sons. Rare talents, combined with unassuming manners and unfailing courtesy, caused Mr Downer to be respected and esteemed alike by friends and acquaintances. Had he possessed the talent without the modesty and graciousness, his career would still have been brilliant and successful, but he would not have taken the firm hold which he undoubtedly gained upon the regard and affection of those with whom he was brought into contact. He took his place in the foremost ranks of the profession not by force of self-assertiveness but by virtue of his extensive and accurate knowledge of the law and his broad grasp of his principles upon which it is

> based; of his keen perceptions which enable him to gain the mastery of a case in an incredibly short space of time; of his possession in an eminent degree of the judicial, in addition to and as distinguished from the purely logical, faculty, by the exercise of which he was able to give their due proportion of weight to the points of an argument and avoid the snares and pitfalls of mere partisan advocacy; and finally of his clear and cogent way of enforcing his view ... His death has left a gap in the profession which it will not be easy to fill: his friends from the first augured for him a brilliant career, and they have not been disappointed ... He has lived long enough to set a bright example to young lawyers, to help to give a high tone to the profession which he adorned, and to collect around him a circle of true friends and a host of admirers ...

The *Advertiser* in its leader wrote:

> By the death of Mr Harold Downer ... South Australia loses one who had within the last few years worked himself into the front rank of the legal profession. Had he but enjoyed the advantage of robust health ... he must before many years have qualified himself for the tenure of the highest positions to which the Bar is an avenue ... South Australia has in proportion to its population a goodly number of members of the legal profession but it is no disrespect to the younger members to say that hitherto none of them has shown themselves to be in possession of talents which will in any way compare with those displayed by the late Mr Harold Downer. His brief but brilliant career won him much well-deserved honour, the memory of which will long serve as a monument to his life.

There was another side to Harold's nature which the conventions of today would countenance more tolerantly than a hundred years ago. When he went up to Cambridge, towards the end of the 1860s, he met Mrs Clay, a relative of his parents. The Clays' daughter, Charlotte Amelia, caught his fancy: a liaison ensued. Some doubt exists as to whether they married, but they must have lived together for some time, for they begat two children: a girl and a boy. Charlotte called herself Mrs

Downner, and their son Harold George bore his father's name. At the time of his birth she resided at Purbrook in Hampshire. Neither she nor the children ever came to Australia. Of what caused the rift between Harold and Charlotte, no evidence remains, but he married no-one else, although there was a hint of a subsequent affair in Victoria. His son Harold George, as will appear in the next chapter, attained considerable distinction in England deprived as he was of a father's guidance and love.

Their daughter, the elder of the two, was christened appropriately Adelaide Amelia Jane. In due course she married Mr Francis George Pope who predeceased her in 1925; Adelaide lived until 22 August 1929. The Popes had only one child, Agnes Nellie. She is now Mrs William Leslie Dixon, a widow whose home is in Dundas, Ontario, Canada, and the mother of several children.

This blemish on Harold's life, despite the encomiums at his passing, reveals an aspect of his character which, as with most of us, falls far below perfection. Yet he was much beloved by his family and his friends. My father used to acclaim him as the cleverest of their generation; his premature end they regarded as tragic; his amours they declined to discuss. There is certainly ample testimony that had he lived a normal span, he might have become, at least in the law, one of Australia's great sons.

## *Chapter 9*

# Frank Haggar Downer, LLB 1863–1938

Most of the preceding chapters have related the lives of men who were both eminent lawyers and public figures. Frank Downer was by profession a solicitor, but neither in the law, politics, nor commerce did he achieve fame as a celebrity. His exploits, in themselves quite remarkable, ranged through other spheres.

The eldest son of HE Downer, he was born at *Hilltop*, Cambelltown on 19 August 1863. He received Haggar as his second name, after his mother Maria's family; from her also he inherited her tall figure, fine features, and good looks. He spent his school days at St Peter's – not that he achieved any memorable distinction as a scholar, but from the first he displayed great prowess at games, soon becoming one of the school's leading athletes. In this and other sporting directions, he was spurred on by his father who at the time, amongst all his other activities, was Master of the Adelaide Hunt Club. With Henry Downer's equestrian skill and example, Frank learnt to ride in his earliest years. No doubt much of his later success in racing, hunting and polo fields originated from his father's tuition. In the result, as sometimes happens, the pupil came to surpass the teacher.

From St Peter's Frank matriculated in 1883, and proceeded to the Adelaide University, where between 1884 and 1887 he studied, obtaining the Final Certificate in Law at the end of that year. On admission to the Bar I am not sure whether at first he entered his father's firm; eventually, however, he joined G & J Downer estate. He worked more on the solicitor's side than the forensic. Public speaking as such never held much attraction for him, and he was much more at ease in the office than in court. He developed a sound judgment, if not an imaginative one, but it is probably true to say that the law never commanded his real interest, or aroused within him an intellectual enthusiasm and devotion without which no man can truly prosper at it.

Frank's contribution to his times was as a sportsman, friend and host. The *Advertiser*, after his death, described him as 'a natural horseman, a fearless rider, and better still a great horse master with an infinite patience when dealing with horses'. When only twenty-four he won his first Hunt Club Cup on his own horse 'Robin Hood', his weight being 12 stone and 7 pounds. Four years later, in 1891, he won again on Uncle George's horse 'Screw-Wrench'. He repeated his success in 1894 and 1895 on his hunter 'Kingfisher'. In these races he was pitted against some of the most accomplished amateurs of the period, and over a course – Morphettville – four miles long intercepted by high fences and a stone wall. In 1935 these old fences and wall were demolished, but the day before, as a final flourish, frank, now aged seventy-two, in company with Miss Phyllis Bray, rode around the course on his horse 'Radiant' to the cheers and delight of his multitude of friends. 'The Downer Handicap', run every year on Adelaide Cup Day, commemorates him.

Hunting appealed to him nearly as much as the turf. He followed his father in being Master of the Adelaide Hunt Club for several years. For a long time he served as a committeeman of the South Australian Jockey club where his advice was valued greatly. But his interest did not stop there. Throughout his adult life he loved polo, where his proficiency as a rider led him to the same triumphs as on the racecourse. On numerous occasions he captained the South Australian Polo Team; he played in many interstate matches and on his various visits to England at Hurlingham. To younger players he was especially kind. Such was his repute that on the day he died, he was captain of the Adelaide Polo Club.

By nature of convivial temperament, Frank enjoyed entertaining, parties, the company of pretty women, and social life. A handsome man, he always kept his slim figure, prided himself on his well-cut clothes, and never allowed his liking for high living to interfere with his physical fitness. One would have thought that such a dashing, debonair, flirtatious temperament would marry some glamorous social beauty with similar interests. Quite the reverse happened. In 1900, when approaching thirty-seven, the bachelor married Miss Charlotte Murray, a sister of GJR Murray who, as Sir George Murray, became one of South Australia's ablest chief Justices and Lieutenant-Governors. Lottie, as her family and friends called her, was tall, rather large, somewhat plain, without flair for smart dressing, but kind, motherly, considerate, with as many facets of splendid character as a Christmas tree has candles. In my childish recollection, she spoke with a rich, plum-cake voice betokening a cultivated mind embodied in worldly well-being. Utterly dissimilar in types, appearance, interest, they provided a paradox of happiness. She understood Frank perfectly; to Lottie he returned all her devotion and affection.

In 1910 Frank and Lottie built a spacious one-storey house at Burnside, set amidst ten or eleven acres where Frank kept his horses. This they called *Hundalee*, after a village in the north of England. In those days they were on the outskirts of Adelaide, enjoying views across to the Hills. To me, as a small boy, the house seemed the last word in modernity, with fitted basins in bedrooms which we never had at Pennington Terrace, tiled bathrooms, and electricity throughout. A huge tiger-skin rug, with head exposing aggressive fangs and glaring glass eyes, lay outstretched in the entrance hall which contained some well-preserved pieces of Downer family furniture from the pioneer days. To the right and left were drawing room and study; a corridor led beyond to the capacious dining room, the scene of many a sumptuous dinner party consisting frequently of several courses. This remained their home always; with enough land to protect it, with quite an elaborate garden, they desired no country retreat. But as with all of us, they suffered disappointments. There were no children. I believe they regretted this sadly. When my father wrote to Frank in November 1909 announcing that my mother was pregnant, he replied (from London): 'I haven't spoken to Lottie about it but I think you had better hand my little cousin over to us and we will try and think it is ours.'

Nor did they share each other's lives for as long as they might expect. Lottie was not a particularly healthy woman and in 1921 she died. Despite his vivacious nature which seemed to demand the company of women, he married no-one else. Almost until the end of his life, he rode every week to the Magill cemetery and placed flowers on her grave.

It would be wrong to think of Frank Downer solely as a noted sportsman and an increasingly disinterested lawyer. Although in politics he stood aside as an observer rather than a participant, he developed some connections with commerce, being a chairman of directors of the local board of Norwich Union Insurance towards the end of his life, as well as a director of some lesser companies. Always a staunch believer in the British Empire, and an upholder of a close Anglo-Australian relationship, he supported actively the Royal Society of St George, being South Australian president when he died. He enjoyed travelling about the world. In England, which he visited from time to time, he made many friends. At the age of sixty-seven, in company with one of his polo colleagues Harold Law-Smith, a well known Adelaide merchant, he undertook an overland tour from Capetown to Cairo and thence on to Palestine. Undaunted on reaching England, he threw himself with spirited vigour into the round of the London season.

He returned to England in 1937, and although well when he sailed in the *Oronsay*, became very ill in London. For some years he thought his heart was causing him trouble, but such indispositions seemed to pass quickly and, as always, he made a joke of them, asking attractive women to hold his hand as he lay momentarily on a sofa. After he came home, his relations were astonished to hear that Adelaide doctors diagnosed his condition as tuberculosis. An operation collapsed one lung, but despite continual cheerfulness, a complete absence of self pity, and much hospitality dispensed from his bedroom, he gradually declined. By now even Frank's zest for living could no longer sustain him, and on 19 March 1938 he died.

*Chapter 10*

# Alderman Sir Harold Downer, LLB 1871–1935

Harold George Downer entered the world without any material advantages. Indeed, in the conventions of the Victorian age his life began under a considerable disadvantage. He was born at *Purbrook*, Hampshire, on 29 October 1971, and on account of his father's desertion was brought up entirely by his mother. Throughout her life she showed character and talent, with devotion to her two children. Harold had much to thank her for; but he was also fortunate in inheriting his father's ability, industry, and love of the law.

He went to the Haberdashers School, founded by one of the ancient London guilds, the Haberdashers. Subsequently he read law at London University where he took his LLB. Apparently he never felt attracted to the Bar, preferring the other branch of the profession. His admission as a solicitor dates from 1896 and he entered the ranks in a cloud of glory, not only with first class honours in the final examinations, but winning the Cliffords Inn and John Mackrell prizes. For the next four years he practised alone. Then in 1900 he formed a partnership with Stanley Johnson (later Sir Stanley Johnson MP), the firm being known as Downer & Johnson, with offices at Salisbury House, London Wall. They remained together until 1928, Johnson in 1918 becoming Conservative MP for the Walthamstow East after two previous unsuccessful attempts.

The year after his admission to practice Harold married. His wife was Elfrida Eldred, a tall, good-looking woman when I first knew her at the end of the 1920s. Originally, they had a religious problem to settle; she was a Roman Catholic, he, as with all Downers, an Anglican. To please her, Harold adopted the Catholic faith, a decision he once told me, he never regretted. 'It is the true faith,' he said. They were very happy together. Freda, as her family called her, gave him warmth, companionship, understanding, and these qualities she radiated to her friends. Hospitable, generous, she helped many in less fortunate circumstances, always exuding motherliness to young people. Her only defect in middle age consisted of a curious impediment in her speech which, when excited, resembled the crowing of a cock. Some people found this embarrassing at first; gradually one became accustomed to it, knowing what to expect. But sometimes strangers were startled. Sadly, this warm-hearted pair produced no children of their own, but in their adopted daughter Joyce they found much recompense.

Although successful professionally, Harold though his many contacts in the City – he became a director of several companies – developed an interest in its administration. The government of the City in conducted by the Corporation of London, consisting of twenty-six Alderman and one hundred and fifty-nine Common Councilmen, all elected by the citizens. The Lord Mayor in turn is elected annually by liverymen from the Aldermen; the two Sheriffs for each year by the liverymen of the eighty-four guilds.

In 1921 Harold became a Common Councilman for Coleman Street Ward. Three years later he had the honour of being elected one of the two Sheriffs for 1924–25. This proved a fascinating and colourful period, with Sir Frederick Barthorpe as his colleague, and Sir Alfred Bower as Lord Mayor. During the year King George V laid the foundation stone of Lloyds; the freedom of the City was presented to a former Prime Minister HH Asquith (by then an Earl); Harold, along with the Lord Mayor and his co-Sheriff visited France on the invitation of the French President following the restoration of devastated Verdun, which the City of London had adopted; whilst the British Empire Exhibition opened at Wembley. The President made him an Officer of the Legion of Honour. More significant, the King knighted him in 1925 at the close of his shrieval term.

Three years later he parted company with Sir Stanley Johnson. Harold by now was fifty-seven, enamoured of the City of London affairs, and with a prospect of loftier eminences. Johnson in 1924 had retired from Parliament, and wished his partner to concentrate more on the law. Dissolution of the firm seemed the best answer. However, in their employ as a salaried solicitor was an able young man named Cyril Lewis who for years had worked on Sir Harold's side of the business, and consequently, as he says, came to know him exceptionally well. These two joined forces a Downer & Lewis, with offices at 111 Moorgate. They agreed that most of the work should be done by Lewis, with Harold to counsel and advise, and to see clients when circumstances required. The new partnership flourished, being as harmonious as it was successful. Harold concentrated increasingly on his civic responsibilities, with Cyril Lewis distinguishing himself as the effective operative partner. Mr Lewis today is a CBE, and though an elderly man still practises at Tunbridge Wells in Kent retaining the old caption Downer & Lewis.

By the time Harold had long enjoyed the distinction of being a Freeman of London through belonging to some of the medieval City companies, he became a member of the Gold and Silver Wyre Drawers, occupying the post of Master for 1931. The Tallow Chandlers, the Loriners, and the Gardeners also acclaimed him as one of their livery. These guilds are justly renowned in England not only for their antiquity but for their philanthropy, most of which is unpublished. Originally all of them were based in halls reminiscent of Oxford and Cambridge; many of these were destroyed by the Great Fire of London in 1665, rebuilt in the elegant richness of Wyre architecture only to be shattered by German bombers during the Second World War. Some, however, still survive, such as the graceful Tallow Chandlers; others have risen again in an idiom combining traditional with contemporary styles. Several times a year the older and more affluent company hold resplendent dinners accompanied by stately ceremonial – dinners which before 1939 were even more elaborate than today. To some of these grand occasions Harold invited me in my Oxford and Bar student years; they formed my introduction to a colourful phase of London life which thirty years later I came to know so well. Once, when he officiated as Master, he made me stand beside him, 'my young cousin from Australia,' to receive the guests. Whenever I was with him at such gatherings, attended as they are by some of the most eminent people in the realm, Harold's popularity and esteem were obvious. Dignified, gracious, always friendly, unpretentious, his success entirely through his own efforts was a delight to behold.

The Harold Downers lived on high ground in the outer parts of South London, Gibson's Hill, not very far from the ill-fated Crystal Palace. It was a comfortable house, without any architectural distinction, called *The Homestead*, with a garden large by the standards of SW16. August and September they spent on the South Coast in their summer house overlooking Poole harbour. His outdoor recreations were sailing and golf, and this part of Dorset provided him with both. In appearance he bore a strong resemblance to the preceding Downer generation: of medium height, broad shoulders, rather straight nose, neither fat nor thin. When I knew him his greying brown hair showed warning signs of thinning on top. He insisted on regular exercise, kept himself in good fettle, resisted the never-ending temptations of London banqueting to eat and drink too much. Doubtless these circumstances, combined with happiness at home, contributed to his robust looks. In conversation he spoke with a slight drawl; his voice, though resonant, descanted none of that clipped English with journalists misdescribe as the Oxford accent. As a public speaker he chose his worlds deliberately, was always effective, but lacked the wit, epigram and originality of phrase that flowed from his uncle Sir John. Whilst conscious of the circumstances surrounding his birth, he was a typical Downer in his *esprit de famille*. And as I saw him, he overflowed in generosity, worked personally in charitable organisations for the relief of those who were sick, poor and destitute and was ever desirous of helping young people.

In 1930 Harold's career took another upward turn. He retired from the Common Council and secured election as an Alderman. This involved him in magisterial duties, for which he soon established a reputation for humanity and compassion. He was also appointed one of His Majesty's Lieutenants for the City of London. But much more stretched before him than that. Upon election to the Court of Aldermen it has long been the custom of the City for a newcomer to await his turn for the coveted prize of Lord Mayor of London. This honour does not befall every Alderman: it comes to most. Harold knew that the panoply, majesty, and responsibility of one of the world's most glamorous offices would be his for the year 1936–37. The Lord Mayor usually is elected early in October; he begins his term towards mid-November. After twelve months of continuous public speaking, feasting, entertaining and being entertained, to say nothing of his considerably judicial, administrative and ceremonial duties, most Lord Mayors thankfully subside into silence and abstinence for the period of their immediate successor. In the 1930s, even more than today, no man could assume the position unless he were able to supplement official allowances from his private funds. For this Harold had provided, setting aside, as he told me £10,000 (equal to at least £50,000 in today's values) of his inheritance form our benefactor Uncle George.

And so often happens in the lives of successful Downers, Fate intervened to deprive him of reaching the summit of his career. One Sunday afternoon, 12 May 1935, Harold and Freda attended a garden party given by their friends of Lord and Lady Ebbisham. Apparently he seemed well, enjoying the occasion. Next day he suddenly felt sick; his doctors rushed him to hospital where they performed an emergency operation for appendicitis. Unhappily, his appendix had burst, necessitating a second operation three days later. Alas! It was all too late. He never rallied and at noon on Friday 17 May his life ended.

At that time, of course, no one could have predicted the events of 1936 and 1937. In January 1936 George V died; in December Edward VIII abdicated. The following year saw the coronation of King George VI and Queen Elizabeth. This was the year Sir Harold Downer would have been Lord Mayor of London. The customary reward in those pre-Wilson and pre-Heath days was a baronetcy for the Lord Mayor; in a coronation year it could have been a peerage. It is sad for all of us who knew and admired Harold that he was denied both the achievement and the reward.

## *Chapter 11*

# John Henry Downer 1872–1911

In terms of achievement, my eldest half brother scarcely deserves a chapter to himself. His all too short life was marred by indifferent health, frustrated hopes, and insufficient resolution. Yet he represents an example of humanity often overlooked by biographers who ever seek to evaluate a man's worthiness by a successful career, his capacity to make money, or his influence on history. John had no career to speak of, made very little money, and contributed nothing to the history of his times. Nevertheless, he is not without importance in our family story. For without achieving anything concrete, his was a personality that made people happy. From accounts of his contemporaries, he exuded unforgettable charm, displayed a kindliness and unselfishness of exceptional depth, possessed a sense of originality and humour of constant delight to his friends, developed a mind of philosophical inquiry which gave him a profundity of insight denied to most whom the worlds calls successful. This was a warm, sensitive, refined should on earth, greatly beloved by his generation.

John H Downer, as he signed himself, was born in Adelaide on 17 July 1872. As with many members of our family he went to St Peter's where his scholastic attainments were considerable especially in the classics. At the age of nineteen, he proceeded to Cambridge; his college was Gonville and Caius, and here he began the study of medicine on 19 April, 1892. Life at Cambridge in the 1890s must have seemed idyllic. His gregarious nature made the most of it, and during vacations he received much hospitality from some of Sir John's friends including the family of Lord Kintore, then Governor of South Australia. But during his third year at Cambridge he suffered his first serious set-back; he became so ill that continuance there became impractical, so he had the mortifying experience of going down without taking a degree. The end of 1894 found him home again; two years later he encountered another blow from his mother's death.

John always remained interested in medicine, but by now he abandoned all intentions of qualifying as a doctor. I believe he used to accompany his father sometimes as a sort of ADC, as at the 1898 Sydney Federal Convention. Apart from that he seems to have spent an indeterminate existence during these post-Cambridge years. Towards the end of the decade, however, an international crisis happened which precipitated him in a direction he had probably never contemplated. This was the outbreak of the Boer War in 1889.

The Downers have never been a military family by inclination or profession, but they volunteer for active service when the occasion demands. The war in South Africa at the turn of the century evoked a remarkable demonstration of loyalty to the throne and to Britain throughout the British Empire, nowhere more so than in Australia. Each colony – or State as it was shortly to become – spontaneously despatched volunteer contingents. John joined the South Australian Light Horse as a trooper, gaining a commission whilst in South Africa. I have always heard his work highly praised, especially his solicitude for the sick and wounded for which his earlier medical studies gave him some qualification. For his services he received a medal (now in my possession) with three bars inscribed 'Cape Colony, Orange Free State, Transvaal.' More valuable was a glowing testimonial by his comrades.

The war ended in 1902, and John returned to Adelaide. He worked sporadically on Uncle John's stations, and not long afterwards that central pillar of the family settled him on *Hawthorndene*, an apple orchard with some grazing land, near Blackwood, which was then a picturesque rural area. Here he resided for what remained of his life.

Despite his liking for girls, and their attraction to him, he never married. They were entranced by his originality, strong, clear-cut features, tall, slim figure, charm of manner, gaiety, with the serious side of his nature relieved by a whimsicality many found appealing. It seems he could not make up his mind to take the final plunge – not, at any rate until he reached thirty-eight: perhaps herein lay his failing in other things. In a sense he was a philanderer. He called his company Downers Affections Unlimited. The women in his life returned their devotion to him until the end of their days. My mother's youngest sister Enid, who in the early 1900s was one of John's inamoratas, loved him, I used to think, more than any other man – despite her own happy, if not altogether satisfying, marriage after his death. The same could be said of others, both in Australia and England. But his last affair could well have given him a wife. The bride-to-be was his cousin Hannah Fulton, a niece of the first Lady Downer. Such a union provoked obvious objections of consanguinity, but not to the singularly felicitous girl of whom all of us were so fond. In 1910 John underwent an operation for a fistula; apparently this set in train something worse. He had long felt intuitively he would not live to be old – there seems to have been a streak of mysticism within him. The next year his condition deteriorated alarmingly. Hannah, who by then had arranged for her wedding dress, offered to marry him at his bedside. John refused, realising no future lay ahead of him in this world. On the last day of June 1911, my mother and father, who were then in London, were handed a cable containing the horrifying news that John had died on the 29 June. Hannah, heartbroken, remained faithful to him in mind and body until her own demise fifty-four years later.

To die before one's thirty-ninth birthday is only half a life. Yet his best friend would not have predicted for John Downer a memorable career. Imbued with little of his father's love of politics and the law, without any pulsating ambition, lacking, it seems, any driving sense of purpose, unwilling to resume his quest for medicine, unattracted by commerce, indifferent to money, he displayed no talents for material success. Nevertheless, he possessed splendid qualities. Primarily, he was a thinker. Widely read in the classics as well as English literature, theology, the incipient subject of psychology, with a taste for science, he was never happier than when talking, discussing, theorising, gently arguing, and mingling with minds of similar bent. To children he showed interest, affection, and understanding – a rare trait in one without any. He was the best-looking man, probably one of the most winsome, endearing personalities our family has produced. And by making people happier for having known him, he enriched his generation and the world in which he moved.

## *Chapter 12*

# James Frederick Downer LLB 1874–1942

~ 1 ~

Sir John's second son, Fred Downer, as he was always known, was born in Adelaide on 5 September 1874. Taller, thinner, better looking than his father, he shared little of his political and legal tastes, although intellectually they had much in common. Temperamentally they differed, as did Fred from his brother John. Each in his own way was strongly individual, united by mutual affection and instinctively similar approaches to the political, social, economic problems of their times. Devoid of any thrusting ambition, still less of any trace of self-seeking by the end of the 1920s Fred had emerged as one of the most prominent, respected figures in the State.

He derived his education from St Peter's College and at Adelaide University. At school he proved himself an all-round boy, good at work and at games. His scholastic success won him several prizes, whilst he displayed extraordinary skills at lacrosse and cricket. He played for the school in both. Horses for him had nothing like the same attraction as for his uncles and cousins, but this aptitude for ball games remained throughout his life. In the Adelaide Club his name recurs frequently as billiards champion; in fact, he became one of the best amateurs in the State. His golfing prowess failed to match his skill at billiards, but his interest induced him to become one of the founders of the Mount Lofty Golf Club forty years on.

His interest in, and devotion to St Peter's never diminished, being constantly concerned with the school's affairs. He never really agreed with my mother's choice of Geelong Grammar for me, for one of his characteristics was not only family loyalty, but loyalty as he conceived it, to institutions with which the family was connected. In his eyes, Geelong and Oxford were inferior educational addresses to St Peter's and Cambridge – just as one's preference for travelling in Orient liners to those of the P & O appeared almost an act of desertion towards a director of Elder Smith who acted for P & O interests in South Australia.

Proceeding on to university he took a law degree, and qualified for admission to the Bar when only twenty-one. Naturally, he began his legal practice in G & J Downer, but the law as a profession made no appeal to him. For some years he edited the *South Australian Law Reports*, a task well-suited to his inquiring and erudite mind. For court work he showed no leaning: he was more at ease as a consultant, which was probably why his career before long diverted to other fields. Uncle George, his father's partner, took a great liking to Fred and reposed deep trust in him. In this way he became the senior AG Downer trustee, and used to have interminable discussions with his uncle about the terms and drafting of this munificent will.

Indeed, the cloak of Elijah fell upon him when AG Downer relinquished his directorship in 1914; the board of Elder Smith turned to Fred, offering him his uncle's vacancy. The following year brought a major re-orientation in his life. After Sir John's death in August 1915, approaches were made to him to stand for his father's seat in the Legislative Council. Fred declined. Politics, he often told me, never held any attraction for him: in his youth he had witnessed so many of the obligations, stresses, financial sacrifices a political career had imposed on 'the Pater'. Nor did he care for the limelight in any form. To his reticent, almost self-effacing nature, publicity was abhorrent. He disliked public speaking; he lacked a clear, commanding voice; personal histrionics were anathema. Yet despite these disqualifications he could make a graceful, well-constructed speech when circumstances compelled. But it was always an effort, undertaken with distaste.

The same year his stars indicated other courses. By the end of 1915 the First World War had advanced to critical dimensions. Aged forty-one, he was considered too old for active service. Nonetheless he ventured into what virtually had become an operational theatre. Elder Smith & Company asked him to become their resident director in London on account of marketing difficulties occasioned by the war, and to this he assented. With his wife and two small children they sailed from Adelaide in the P & O *Maloja*, the newest and largest ship of the line, on a voyage not free from hazards.

By this time Fred had enjoyed a serene domestic existence for some years, marred only by two sadnesses which left a mark subsequent achievement never erased. In 1902 he had married Florence Way Cambell, four years his senior: she was a daughter of a well-known Adelaide doctor, Allen Cambell, whilst her mother was a sister of the Chief Justice and Lieutenant-Governor, Sir Samuel Way. Florrie was petite, energetic, wiry, high-principled with a streak of ascetism in her composition springing perhaps from her nonconformist Way forbears. In her youth she must have looked pretty without being beautiful, with delicate, refined features reminiscent of a Dresden china figure. Intensely musical, she made local history by being the first woman to gain a Mus Bac. At the Adelaide University as a pianist, she won high appreciation far and wide. By nature shy, she cared little for the social world as she grew older; but although some people found her reserved she showed a friendly manner relaxing to a point of animation with those whom she felt an accord. Her life revolved around her husband, children, relations, gardens and houses – in that order. And her over-riding interest centred in children – not just her own but other people's.

It was in their love for children that Fred and Florrie encountered tragedy. Their first child, Elizabeth Florence, born on May Day 1906, died three weeks later. Their second girl Alleyne Joan followed the next year on 7 May. She lived to marry Henry Rymill but died suddenly in April 1942, the day after her third baby was born. The Fred Downers' third child, Sidney Frederick, born on 16 September 1909, outlived both his parents, but he was the only to do so. In 1911 they had another son, John, who survived until only two and a half. Thus they lived to see three of their four children predecease them. The loss of Alleyne, healthy, strong, accomplished, public-spirited, at the age of thirty-five was the bitterest blow of all.

Fred and his family stayed in England from towards the end of 1915 until 1919. He took a house at Berkhamsted, twenty-six miles north-east of London, mainly in the children's interests to diminish danger from German air raids. Britain's excellent railway services, then in some respects better than now, enabled him to commute rapidly to his office in the City. Both he and Florrie threw themselves energetically into auxiliary activities, providing open house for Australian troops on leave. His sound business judgment proved of enormous benefit to Elder Smith, particularly in helping to surmount problems concerning the sale and shipment of Australian wool, wheat and metals. Billy Hughes, Australia's famous war Prime Minister, was glad to consult him on his London visits in 1916 and 1918. During the Peace Conference in Paris in 1919, Hughes asked Fred to join his delegation for part of the negotiations.

He obviously did well in England, and accomplished much on Australia's behalf. Despite unprecedented difficulties, exceeded only by the crisis of 1939–45, he enjoyed British life except that he found many Englishmen with whom he had to deal arrogant, condescending, and rather grand. By the end of 1919 he was glad to return home and resume his interests in South Australia which, as with the rest of our continent, had suffered less from the war – apart from the irreparable slaughter of 60,000 Australian youths – than any other belligerent of comparable importance.

He had pleasant places awaiting him. After his marriage his father had given him *Prospect House*, a single-storeyed building with spacious room on the corner of Pennington Terrace and Palmer Place. Its lack of architectural appeal was compensated by commanding views over the park, the city of Adelaide, and the Mount Lofty Ranges beyond; on the western side lay the lawns and trees of Palmer Place flanked opposite by *Montefiore*, the home of Florrie's Uncle Samuel. Much of this has now gone. In the 1960s, *Prospect House* fell to the demolisher's hand; in its stead rose a nondescript block of doctors' consulting rooms. For many years St Thomas Aquinas Roman Catholic College transformed the house of that staunch evangelical Bible Christian, Sir Samuel Way.

In the Hills, *Glenalta* beckoned. Part of the estate belonged to him already, again his father's gift. In 1920 my mother, who by then had re-married, relinquished for a modest sum her right to the house, thus providing Fred with complete ownership. Thence forth *Glenalta* increasingly became his principal home. Both he and Florrie were ardent gardeners: within a few years they doubled the extent of *Glenalta's* garden, added more rooms; finally in 1935 engaged in a virtual redesign of the house by superimposing a second storey. In this enchanting woodland setting, they joyfully toiled in whatever spare time they could seize. Nor were their children overlooked. A tennis court, cricket pitch, swimming pool in the old fernery gave much delight to them and their friends – but no trace of these youthful embellishments remains.

Other commercial successes came his way. In 1927 he joined the board of *The Adelaide Electric Supply Company* where his legal knowledge and commercial sense met with instant appreciation. Nineteen years later, when the South Australian Government nationalised this undertaking, and when the Premier, Sir Thomas Playford, appointed me to the first board. I heard nothing but the highest praise of Fred from senior officers. The Commercial Union Insurance Company made him one of its directors, and in 1929 a more engrossing and more interesting opportunity arose with the reorganisation of the *Advertiser* newspaper. The proprietor of that journal since 1893 had been Sir Langdon Bonython who, besides being a remarkable journalist, served in the two first Commonwealth Parliaments, and over a long life proved to be one of the State's most generous benefactors. At the age of eighty he sold most of his interest to a new company called *Advertiser Newspapers Limited*, in which the *Melbourne Herald* and the *Weekly Times* took thirty-seven per cent of the shares; the remainder were offered to the public. Fred accepted the position of chairman of directors of this new concern. Sir Keith Murdoch, head of the Herald group, represented Melbourne interests, and so began a firm friendship which over flowed to younger members of the family such as myself. I have met many journalists and newspaper proprietors in my life in England, Australia, and elsewhere; none of them has equalled Keith Murdoch for dynamism, strength of personality, charm of manner or impressive appearance. A controversial character, people either praised or detested him. So far, he had had no successors of the same luminosity in Australia, nor in any contemporary British newspaper figure his equal.

The *Advertiser*, with its many ramifications, absorbed a large slice of Fred's time. He and Murdoch made a splendid initial choice for the managing editor in the person of Lloyd Dumas. Dumas, seventeen years Fred's junior, was born at Mount Barker, South Australia; his father started what is still a lively informative outspoken, local publication, the *Mount Barker Courier*. By 1929 he had attained a wide variety of journalistic experience in London and Melbourne. At the relatively young age of thirty-eight, he brought many talents to the *Advertiser*; next to Keith Murdoch, I would place Sir Lloyd, as he eventually became, in the ranks of truly great journalists. Inevitably, Lloyd and Fred saw much of each other: they, too, became close friends, despite their differences in background, tastes and personality. To the end of his life – he died in 1973 – Dumas spoke warmly of Fred's friendship, guidance and assistance.

I think he always realised that Fred provided him with the springboard for his great opportunities.

These two men shared one attribute in common: a generous and kindly heart. Everyone who worked in the *Advertiser* network during the thirteen years of the Downer-Dumas duumvirate knew this. Fred's most attractive attribute was his sympathy for those less fortunate than himself, his constant concern for the underdog. There were plenty of occasions for the exercise of this in the years following the advent of the new company. As 1929 progressed, the shadows of the Great Depression encompassed the world. Australia suffered severely with financial stringency, unemployment, low wages, for many investor no dividends. But the *Advertiser* weathered the storm better than most. By the mid 1930s its news coverage, literacy standards, leading articles and general presentation gave it a more persuasive influence with pubic opinion than it exerts today.

Another top position was to be his, but not until 1941 when only one more year of his life remained. Appropriately, his old company, Elder Smith, made him chairman after the death of Mr Tom Elder Barr Smith – a gentleman in every sense of the word who, to his contemporaries and many of us younger men, seemed the finest flower of his generation. Fred appreciated the compliment: the family connection with Elders dated from the 1880s; but the world was then in the trough of the Second World War and the allies beset by difficulties of unimagined magnitude.

Moreover, he knew that his days were shortening. In 1939, after several months when he noticeably aged, he suddenly announced he had to enter hospital for a major operation. Fred had always looked a reasonably healthy person. His slim appearance never deserted him, he exercised regularly and he ate and drank in strict moderation. In 1927 he suffered from skin irritation for such a degree that he went to London expressly to consult with doctors, and on that occasion succumbed to such a wave of pessimism that he presented a large slice of his library to the Adelaide Club. His highly strung temperament let him to fear for the worst, remembering that his mother, elder brother, and father had died from cancer. He returned reassured, but uncured of his skin affliction. This he never lost and people who complained sometimes of his surprising bursts of irritability without apparent cause did not know the discomfort he ever tried to conceal. But the doctors' verdict of 1939 confirmed his dire apprehensions: they advised an immediate operation to arrest cancer in the bowel. The die being cast, he faced the ordeal cheerfully; he always showed plenty of courage; but such drastic surgery diminished his strength, brought in its train physical inconvenience which he bravely bore, and postponed merely for three years the inevitable end.

Apart from national and international problems of the war which, of course, worried him deeply, and his failing health, other anxieties afflicted him. In 1940 his son Sidney had enlisted in the Royal Air Force in England. The following year he was posted to South East Asia. Japan's treacherous attack on Pearl Harbour on 8 December 1941 ignited the war in Asia. Within two months her armies, navy, and air force had swept as far south as Singapore. In March, Java fell and though Sidney had managed to escape from Singapore he was taken prisoner in Java, though whether Fred ever knew he had survived is doubtful. Personnel reported missing in confrontation with so savage a foe do not comprise a subject of hopeful conjecture. By now Fred was declining alarmingly. An even worse tragedy befell him towards the end of April. His daughter, Alleyne Rymill, whom he adored, and whom he rightly regarded as the stronger character of his two children, provided a shaft of sunlight when she gave birth to her third baby, a girl on 22 April. No complications attended her confinement. A sturdy young woman, she radiated physical and mental well-being. In hospital the next day, whilst sitting up in bed, she suddenly gave a sigh, and was gone. A blood clot, the doctors said, a million to one chance. The blow proved still more crushing to Florrie, to whom Alleyne was daughter, best friend, confidante, and from whom she could gain succour with the sorrowful prospects of widowhood, and the uncertain fate of her son. Poor Florrie, it was almost too much for her iron determination to bear. She lived for another nineteen years, finding fleeting solace in her grandchildren, a gently decaying shadow of her former self, gradually sinking into senility, in her rational moments, constantly reliving her life with Fred.

For him the end came mercifully on 29 May, 1942. It was a cruel close to a good innings, played over sixty-seven years. By the standards of the world he had achieved much. Born with many talents, he developed them to advantage. Had he been more ambitious, success could have been glittering. His well-attuned mind fitted him for many pursuits. Hit literary tastes were Catholic in range, with a preference for history, biography, books on politics, leading nineteenth and twentieth century English authors. American history and affairs seemed to fascinate him, but for instant relaxation he would read the latest novel or detective story. As with most Downers he was prone to intolerance on matters he did not sufficiently understand or towards those with whom he disagreed. He felt things deeply. There was a strong undercurrent of emotion within him which could flash into aggressive indignation if he were thwarted. His daily life flowed in orderly sequence. Well-disciplined, methodical, industrious, he displayed scant patience with those who were lazy. Meticulous punctuality he insisted upon, as on two occasions I discovered to my cost. He enjoyed the company of young people, and his homes were always open to his children's friends. His own children he idolised. No doubt the loss of them in infancy contributed to an exaggerated consideration of the interests and welfare of the survivors. Neither of them, it seemed to me, returned in full the affection he heaped on them. Yes, they respected him, admired many of his standards and his traits, yet in numerous ways they hurt his sensitive nature.

It is a hard thing to say, but his generous nature overlooked too much towards them. Had he been less indulgent, his son might have made a richer contribution when deprived of his example and guidance.

Fred made many friends but few intimates. His relations were fond of him, though at times they found him unpredictable in his views. His loyalty to the family in its widest sense was unswerving, but he tarnished his warm and kindly nature occasionally by personal criticisms which wounded. He was not an easy person to grow close to: however one persevered, he seemed to hold you at arm's length. Perhaps the fault lay in me, thirty-six years younger: whatever the reason, the gap is one I shall ever regret having been unable to bridge. He was instinctively courteous, gracious in manner, with a quiet charm enlivened by humour and anecdotes. Not even his critics – for a man of such forthright convictions could not escape opposition – could dispute his lofty principles and his over-riding should of honour. My father-in-law Sir James Gosse disliked him heartedly, and the sentiment was returned. Personal publicity, exhibitionism, any parade of virtues, he detested. Only the recipients knew his unceasing acts of kindness; children educations, annuities to those in need, donations to cause which touched his heart.

He was not a religious man in any conventional sense. The Church, as an institution, made no appeal to him. Parsons were a species of humanity he could respect but cared for little. 'We believe what we want to believe,' he once said to me. He gave one the impression of being sceptic; if he entertained a religious faith he never discussed it. What his ultimate beliefs were I do not know. But if there is any meaning in language he was a good man in the sight of God when his spirit finally emerged from that decaying body on that May evening the trumpets would surely have sounded for him on the other side, even though perhaps he could scarcely comprehend the sphere of Light and Love which was his due.

~ 2 ~

Something must now be said about the Fred Downers' descendants.

Their children, Alleyne and Sidney, each possessed strong personality, but a more diverse brother and sister it would be hard to find. In character and appearance they bore little resemblance. Sidney was tall, exceptionally good-looking in his twenties, smooth, quick-witted, charming, companionable, generous, emotional, modest. He could also suddenly become vitriolic, mentally cruel, moody, hyper-critical, and detestable. To spend a day with Sidney was like a Mediterranean cruise: you would have plenty of sunshine, relaxation, laughter, always something good to look at. Then, without warning, the sky would blacken, the wind would howl, the sea would rise – and you would search hurriedly for the nearest haven. Alleyne, on the contrary, shared few of Sidney's physical advantages. Rather dumpy in figure, she lacked animation, nor did her fine brain and intellectual gifts show themselves in ease of manner. She looked at life with serious intent, read widely, at school worked hard and successfully, and displayed laudable public spirit.

There were many aspects of her which I admired. Stable as the Rock of Gibraltar, she was a magnificent friend. Although superficially, when younger, almost a blue-stocking – in truth she was very clever and would have made an able lawyer or doctor – she remained essentially a woman; and her happy, all too short marriage with Henry Rymill brought out her latent femininity to full flower. Marriage, indeed, transmitted her in a way I have seen happen to no other girl. She quickly developed more interest in her clothes, acquired as if by magic a dress sense, revealed a conversational skill hitherto suppressed, adored her husband and her children. They were married in St Peter's College Chapel on 26 September 1934, with a reception afterwards on the terraces of *Glenalta*. Henry complimented me, recently arrived from England, by asking me to be his best man. The speech this necessitated, preceded by inward terror, was my first in South Australia.

Such a union produced gladness all round. The Rymills and Fred Downers were old friends, particularly Henry's mother Shylie, a daughter of Lady Way by her first marriage, and therefore a connection of Florrie's. The bridegroom was the sort of man any other father would be proud to acclaim as a son-in-law. Works manager of General Motors-Holden at an early age, he devoted many of his out of office hours to public service, notably the Boy Scout movement, eventually rising to be Chief Commissioner for Australia. In 1949 he received a CPE; had he lived longer he might well have been knighted. They had three children: the eldest Henry, a stockbroker, who with his wife and family subsequently lived at *Glenalta*; their eldest girl Margaret, the wife of James Forwood; the youngest daughter named after her mother and nicknamed 'Lalla', is as yet unaccountably unmarried. Henry Rymill's activities as a Scout Leader were matched by Alleyne in the Girl Guides. When she died she had given great leadership for some time as South Australia Commissioner. Henry outlived her for nearly twenty-nine years. Eventually he married an old friend Barbara Randell in 1967, but their happiness was shattered by his sudden death in Sydney four years later at an international scout jamboree. His enjoyment of social life, his liberality as a host, his love of yachting, allied with his more serious activities, won for him popularity and respect throughout Australia. At the age of sixty-three Adelaide lost one of its most esteemed figures.

Sidney Downer followed his father and grand-father to St Peter's. His native intelligence and rapidity of apprehension enabled him to achieve all that was required in passing examinations; his father's constant interest, and coaching, contributed in no small measure to his academic distinction. Naturally good at games, his addiction to cricket from very early years became a major preoccupation throughout his life. Not surprisingly, he captained the school eleven, leading his team to a series of matches in Ceylon during his final year. Had he remained in South Australia, he would probably have played for the State. From St Peter's he went up to Trinity College, Cambridge, in October 1928. There he met with disappointment in missing out on inclusion in the university team. But he found other compensations in that seductive atmosphere, and had the misfortune not to pass his first year's examinations the following June. Even in the 1920s when university entrance was considerably easier than today, both Oxford and Cambridge insisted on undergraduates jumping this hurdle. Inability to do so resulted in being sent down. Unfortunately Sidney suffered this fate, and his father, disappointed and irritated, ordered him back to Australia.

It was then he decided on journalism as a career. He began working with the *Melbourne Herald* in 1930, and on this lively, provocative, informative newspaper – still I believe, the best afternoon newspaper in the world – gained varied experience under the kindly surveillance of Keith Murdoch for the next three years. During this period he met the girl who was to be his first wife, and the mother of his two children: Melbe Roark, daughter of a Melbourne stockbroker. They were married in 1932, Sidney being only twenty-two, Melbe approaching twenty-six. When I first knew her two years later she looked pretty, had an attractive manner, talked easily and sympathetically possessed a beautiful figure. She reminded me of a musical comedy actress of the time, Lady June Inverclyde, then one of the toasts of London. She is still a very good looking woman. Alas, their happiness was not to last, but after Sidney's move to the *Adelaide Advertiser* in 1933, their children were born – John William in 1935, Elizabeth Melbe in 1937.

After the outbreak of war in 1939, Sidney was posted to *Australian Associated Press* in London. In 1940 he joined the RAF and his wife returned to her children in Australia. The end of 1941 – he had progressed to Flight-Lieutenant – found him in Singapore. In February 1942 he and others made a hair-railing escape in a 5000 ton Chinese freighter. Eventually the party reached Java, but brave as was the attempt to elude the clutches of the Japanese so as to be of use elsewhere, their efforts proved unavailing. Java fell and Sidney became a prisoner. For the next three and a half years he suffered the vicissitudes common to all Japan's prisoners-of-war. His officer's status shielded him from some of the worst indignities, but he had the misfortune to be shifted in the holds of Japanese cargo vessels from Java to Singapore – where I saw him briefly when he passed through Changi – and from thence to Formosa. Again he was moved, this time to Manchuria where he met with intense hardships. And there he regained freedom when the war ended.

Being in the British service, Sidney elected for repatriation to England which he reached in the northern autumn of 1945. He remained there throughout 1946, recovering his health, and adjusting himself to civilian life and the new world emerging, working for a while in the Air Ministry. By now he felt his marriage had collapsed. However, in response to entreaties from his mother and friends (including myself) he resolved half-heartedly to attempt reconciliation. I met him at the Adelaide railway station on Christmas morning 1946, in sweltering heat; he looked well, and was in one of his combative moods. Two months later he and his wife parted. Clearly, their former affection lay amongst the innumerably war casualties of this kind.

He settled easily into the life of Adelaide, for which despite his British proclivities, he always held a strong sentiment. Sir Lloyd Dumas, ever mindful of Fred's friendship, welcomed him back to the *Advertiser*. That he did not make more of his opportunities was through no fault of Dumas. Soon he found a new love in the person of Mrs Margaret Dutton, a widow of about his own age, a daughter of Major VM Newland MP, and a grand-daughter of Simpson Newland, one of Sir John's ministers in 1885. She is one of my oldest friends so, of course,

I am prejudiced in her favour. Both physically and mentally she attracted Sidney passionately. This is not surprising, as she combined beauty with intelligence, social grace with international outlook. On 8 September 1948 they were married. By a coincidence, that same afternoon on our way to the wedding reception, I nominated for Liberal party pre-selection for the House of Representatives seat of Angas. Hurriedly throwing a mackintosh over my morning suit lest seeing a parliamentary candidate so attired would confirm my opponents' worst suspicions, I threaded my way across North Terrace traffic, dodging a hearse which ominously had stopped directly in front of the Liberal and Country League offices – a grave portent, I thought – but for whom? For my political future, or Sidney's second marriage?

It was a portent for the latter. Had they fallen in love twenty years previously, his life might have been more fruitful. At first the sun shone as on a spring morning. Margaret encouraged him with his work, and her own literary bent stimulated the writing of his first book, *Patrol Indefinite*, an account of the Northern Territory Mounted Police (1963). This covered unbroken ground, is a valuable contribution to the history of an insufficiently known part of Australia, and is written with the pleasant easy style which Sidney commanded. But domestic harmony lasted only a few years. Two such decided personalities in middle age found living together under the same roof increasingly difficult. By 1962 they had separated and divorce proceedings began.

For Sidney, married life with its accompanying compromises, was something which he demanded but found hard to achieve. Some men can live without a woman; he could not. His next association was an essay in femininity of a different mould. Before the final rupture with Margaret, he became entranced by Mrs Dorothy Anderson, a member of the old established Clampett family, who years before had been compelled to divorce her husband. Of all his liaisons this was to prove the happiest. Sidney's loves were always good-looking with figures which many a model would envy. Doss, as she was known, had more. Her talents with him were gentleness, understanding, forbearance, and intuition about when to keep silent and when to argue. An accomplished hostess, with two girls of her own, she loved him for his strength and charm, and tolerated his weaknesses. He would be the first to acclaim that her loyalty and devotion to him were beyond all praise. They were married in 1964, and lived in his old house on Fitzroy Terrace.

By now he was starting to age prematurely. Not that he lacked exercise – he was too fond of games to neglect his physical condition; but since a boy he had preferred to burn the candle at both ends, and this coupled with mental and bodily stresses of the war years started to take a toll. One of his legs caused him pain and disability; then his eyes became afflicted with cataracts, necessitating two operations. All the while he had commenced his second book, *100 Not Out: A century of cricked on the Adelaide Oval.* Regrettably, he did not live to see it published – this could not be until 1972 – because in September 1969 whilst in hospital battling with pneumonia, his heart suddenly gave way, and without warning he died a few days after his sixtieth birthday.

Sidney Downer made many friends, and as with all men who act on impulse, and unconventionally, a few enemies. Born with an acute brain, swift insight, every conceivable family and social advantage, he could have achieved much for his country, his family, and himself had he developed more determination, fixity of purpose, a stronger single-mindedness, better judgment. His quarrelsome nature did not despoil the affection many of us felt for his other qualities. My lamentation is that by failing to extricate himself from his own weaknesses, he denied himself the high success for which he was so abundantly equipped.

Sidney left an admirable legacy in his progeny. John William, now a man in his forties, and bearing the names of his distinguished great-grandfather, became one of the fourth generation of Downers to go to St Peter's. As with his father he did well in work and sport, attracting personal popularity. From school he studied at Adelaide University where he took a degree in engineering. At first he worked in Melbourne, where he met Christine Whitehead, daughter of a grazier in the Riverina: they were married in November 1964, but divorced in 1976. Early in his career he joined the world-wide engineering organisation of Maunsell & Company, and this led him to Canberra, several years in London, then to Singapore. He is now a partner in Maunsell's Australian company, and for some time has been stationed at Hong Kong, carrying heavy responsibility for the whole of their operations in South-East Asia (here he met his present wife Rose, who he married in 1979). An assiduous worker, he knows how to relax, and his quiet sense of humour, together with a handsome appearance heightened by personal charm, augur well for his future. As Maunsell's principal representative in a region so vital to Australia, he has acquired a knowledge of our northern neighbours in many respects more intimate than that of some Australian diplomats. Being a man of many interest, besides possessing a European as well as Asian outlook, it is to be hoped that his counsel will be sought by imaginative Australian Governments. They are in need of it.

Elizabeth, Sidney's daughter, inherited her father and mother's good looks. She married first William Davidson, a grazier in the southern Hills, who belongs to a family long settle in South Australia. They have three children. She is now the wife of Reginald Tolley, and lives a happy and useful life in Adelaide.

Alick, 9 months old

Sir John Downer and his wife Una Downer
with a friend at Glenalta, 1910

Alick and Sir John Downer, 1910

Alick with his mother Una Addison, 1930s

Alick and Mary on their wedding day, 1947

Alick, now the Minister of Immigration, and Mary
at Adelaide Airport, 1958

*Arbury Park*, 1950s

Alick, 1964

Alick and Mary with their children Angela, Alexander, Una and Stella
at *Arbury Park*, 1964

Alick with Angela, Stella, Una and Alexander, 1964

Alick and Mary outside Australia House in London, 1960s

Mary Downer with Sir Robert Menzies on a visit to London, 1960s

Alick, Mary and the Queen Mother, 1960s

Alick with the Lord Mayor of London. Every year the Australian dried fruit industry produced a Christmas pudding to present to the city of London to be distributed to those less fortunate, 1960s

Alick at the launching of the Australian Fruit Company, London, 1965

Alick and Mary at Stoke Lodge, the official residence of the Australian High Commissioner is London, 1970s. The painting is a portrait of Mary by Ivor Hele

Alexander Downer with his children Olivia and Georgina (his sister Una is in the background), 1982

Mary Downer on her 80th birthday with her children,
Alexander, Una, Angela and Stella, 2004

Mary with her family: Alexander Downer, Tom Lawrence, Bertie Stephens, Una Lawrence (née Downer), Bob Lawrence, Nicky Downer, Angela Moensch (née Downer), Joanna Lawrence, Edward Downer, Stella Downer, Henrietta Downer, Patrick O'Neil, Olivia Downer, Georgina Downer, 2004

*Chapter 13*

# The Hon Sir Alexander Downer KBE, LLD, MA 1910–1981

~ 1 ~

Reluctantly, but only for the record, I must write something about myself.

I was born on 7 April 1910 in my father's Adelaide house, then designated 42 Pennington Terrace now St Mark's College of the Adelaide University. Sir John was then approaching sixty-six, my mother thirty-nine. It was a spacious Victorian home: my parents' bedroom, (wherein I entered the world) and my nursery both overlooked the park. My early childhood, in retrospect, seems ideally happy – a loving mother and father, kindly nurses, affectionate relatives. Every summer and early autumn we lived at *Glenalta*, my father's country house in the Hills. This to me was bliss. Here I quickly developed a love for the Mount Lofty Ranges which I will never lose.

My father's death in August 1915 altered this equable existence. To assuage her grief my mother and I sailed for Egypt in November in the P & O *Mongolia*. Her youngest sister Enid and her brother-in-law Richard Moser, a civil engineer, were living in Cairo, also my grandfather Henry Russell. For a child the voyage proved exciting. Being at war with Germany, the ship's lower deck was given over to units of the AIF bound for the Middle East. There was a partial black-out at night, for although the Indian Ocean in those years was virtually a British lake, merchant ships had to guard against the *ménage* of German raiders. I shall never forget passing through the Suez Canal to Port Said, the banks lined by British and Australian troops, the passengers throwing them tins of cigarettes and other things. In Cairo we remained five months in my uncle's pleasant house on Gezireh with a garden sloping down to the Nile. To this day I have some nostalgia for Cairo. Despite all the changes of the century, whenever I return there a sense of familiarity remains.

Back in Adelaide in 1916, my mother took a flat at the Grand Central Hotel for a few months, Pennington Terrace having been let to the Manager of the bank of Adelaide and his deliciously eccentric wife Mrs Shields. The Grand Central alas is no more, having now given way to a multi-storey car park. I shall always associate it with listening to the first of the unending series of public speeches I was destined to hear, when WM Hughes, Prime Minister of Australia, made a rousing oration in the hotel dining room at a luncheon given him on his return from London in 1916. The effect on the audience was electric. They rose to their feet, sang 'For he's a jolly good fellow,' all of which so impressed this child of six that I said to my mother, 'That's what I want to do some day.'

The next three years developed into a phase of much travelling within Australia, with two unpleasant episodes. In 1917, Adelaide surgeon Dr Cudmore (later Sir Arthur) removed my appendix, and six months later I underwent a much more serious operation on my back by Sir Alexander MacCormick, the noted Sydney surgeon. Most of 1918 we spent in Sydney, where I went to my first substantive school, Edgecliff Preparatory. There, to my surprise, I achieved my first academic distinction with a prize for Dictation.

The year 1919 saw another dramatic change in my life. In February my mother married D'Arcy Wentworth Addison, of Hobart, Tasmania. This involved settling in Hobart, which to my juvenescent mind seemed small, cold and remote. A bachelor of forty-seven who, until then, had been the mainstay of his family, my step-father was a man of ability, the highest principles, and much kindness of heart. His attitude towards me was that of a devoted parent, but in many respects he could not have contrasted more with my father. At that time he occupied the post of Under-Secretary, virtually the head of the Tasmanian Civil Service. He belonged to a pioneer family, related to the Wentworths of New South Wales; his father had been a captain in the Royal Irish Lancers, and a military attaché at the British Embassy in Brussels. His mother, an old lady of penetrating tenderness, came from Jersey. Despite his international associations, my step-father was the most patriotic, perfervid Tasmanian one could find. This evoked in me all my latent South Australian feelings. Hobart, although beautiful, seemed like exile. It could never be home. Yet I am immensely grateful for the guidance, advice, and affection this good man gave me throughout his life. It is a debt I can never repay.

In Hobart I was sent to my next major school, Hutchins. On the whole I enjoyed those years between 1920 and 1923. My initial period was interrupted by serious illness, followed by a vivid trip to Hong Kong and Japan with my parents, lasting six months. Being by then an impressionable boy of ten, this journey still seems so clear as if it were merely a few years past. In the 1940s, during my life as a prisoner-of-war of the Japanese, the three months we stayed in Japan served as some mental corrective to the brutalities of our captors. Six weeks in Hong Kong during December 1920 to January 1921 instilled in me a love for that beautiful place which even today's high-rise buildings, allied to the fantastic growth in its population, cannon erase.

Although academically I did well at Hutchins, my mother wished me to grow up an Australian rather than belonging to a particular State. So in February 1924 I began my four years at Geelong Grammar. A day boy at Hutchins, the transition to life at what was then a Spartan boarding school, proved difficult and hateful. For at Hutchins, from the age of twelve I suddenly learnt to love work for work's sake. This undoubtedly was due to two gifted schoolmasters, Mr LC Russell and Mr Waring. One of my friendly rivals in the latter's form was Stan Burbury, eventually to become Sir Stanley Burbury, KCVO, KBE, Chief Justice of Tasmania and Governor of Tasmania from 1973 to 1981. Gradually, however, I adjusted to Geelong. There were occasional holidays in Adelaide which were joyous, though mostly I returned to Tasmania in either of the notorious little ships *Loongana* or *Nairans,* sometimes experiencing the worst sea crossings in my long association with the sea. But by 1926 I had made a number of school friends which remained forever; my work, after setbacks which gave me severe and necessary mortification, started to improve; by the end of 1927 I had achieved the academic successes and prizes that my mother expected of me, and so without any real regret my school-days ended. Unfortunately, whatever capacity I showed in the classroom was not reflected in games. Cricket and football I disliked; athletics were fun; rowing was pleasurable. These defects were serious disadvantages at a public school such as Geelong in the 1920s. Yet my years there, with periods of unhappiness, the windy, bleak, often bitter Corio weather, the unattractive landscape, inoculated me to withstand subsequent vicissitudes in a highly salutary manner. And boys of my generation were fortunate in that stern, unbending, ascetic ecclesiastic Dr Francis Brown, the headmaster. I think of him often as one of the moulding moral influences of my life. I was fortunate, too, in my English and History master Eric Nall, whose imaginative tuition prepared me so much for what I was about to discover in Europe, as well as my first year at Oxford.

~ 2 ~

My adult life dawned in 1928. My mother considered it would be wise for me to see something of Europe and England before going up to Oxford in October, so we sailed in the Orient liner *Otranto* on 3 March, disembarking at Naples four weeks later. It was in Naples I had my eighteenth birthday; here began my love for Italy, which continues to grow with the years. Rome, Florence, Milan, Venice, Lake Como, followed in leisurely succession; thence to Lucerne, Paris and London on the verge of summer. From a flat in what is now called the Kensington Palace Hotel, overlooking Kensington Gardens, one came to know the England of George V, Stanley Baldwin, Ramsay MacDonald: an England which was still the centre of a great empire, where manners were formal, class differences rigid, living cost compared with fifty years later, unbelievably cheap. My mother's second sister Ethel and her husband Sam Brittain, a retired engineer, lived in a pretty seventeenth century farmhouse in Gloucestershire; their kindness to me made this a sort of home. Another Continental excursion in the early autumn, to the Low Countries and Germany preceded my initiation to Oxford in Michaelmas term.

Dr Brown recommended my trying for Brasenose, which then valued its Australian connection – Dr Sampson, the principal, and he were old friends. I had set my heart on taking the new course of Politics, Philosophy, Economics, with modern British History appended, together with French and Italian. The principal tried to dissuade me, saying frankly BNC was not equipped for such an embryonic faculty. But bent on a political career, I persisted. He let me have my way; later I realised the correctness of his judgment. Helpful as the dons were, they were not geared to an honours school of this nature. I never regretted my determination; for my public life these subjects provided an intellectual background which is still enormously valuable; but despite some promising successes, in interim college examinations, I was devastated in my university finals narrowly to miss a second class (that would have been bad enough) and to see my name only with a third class honour. After taking my BA degree I remained at Oxford for a fourth year, to read for a post-graduate diploma in Economics and Political Science. This was really an extension of PPE; it also provided an excuse for lingering amidst the enchantments of those dreaming spires until June 1932.

These undergraduate years were enhanced by fortuitous

circumstances. During 1930 and 1931 my stepfather represented Tasmania in Britain as Agent-General, a post he adorned with distinction. He and my mother rented a charming house at 8 Granley Place SW7, a happy home for me where frequently they welcomed my university friends. Their official position enabled me to meet a variety of public personages which otherwise would not have been possible: my step-father was always most generous in the opportunities he deliberately gave me. Ill-health prevented him from continuing beyond the northern autumn of 1931, and towards the end of that year they sailed for Australia. I met them in Adelaide, having spent the summer vacation journeying (in the famous *Mauritania)* to America, Canada, and thence southwards to visit my relations in South Australia. More important, as my mother urged me, now that I had turned twenty-one, and entered into my inheritance from the family benefactor Uncle George, it was necessary to assume control of my affairs. This entailed missing the first term of my Diploma Course, but back at Oxford in January 1932, and still smarting from my examination disappointment six months earlier, the incentives were strong to double one's efforts.

Much had been written about Oxford in the 1920s and 1930s and this is not the place to add it. A little, however, I must say on a personal note. The effect of those four years on my mental unfolding was profound. The lecturers were of uneven quality. Those who influenced me most were WGS Adams of All Souls Gladstone, Professor Political Theory; Sir Reginald Coupland, Beit Professor of History of the British Empire; the socialist economist GDG Cole; the economic historian E Lipson; and Dr William Brown, a philosopher. Adams, Coupland and Cole were a delight to listen to, delivering their lectures as speeches, striding up and down the dais with captivating eloquence. Cole made no attempt at impartiality: one of his favourite targets was Churchill, who had just ceased to be Chancellor of the Exchequer, but his provocation, no doubt, was deliberate as a stimulus to thought. Lipson, small and pronouncedly Jewish in appearance, read his lectures, but of such quality that he held his crowded audiences in rapt attention.

I made some splendid friends. Opportunities abounded for political activity, both through the Oxford Union and the University Conservative Association. At Union debates one heard the leading statesmen of the day: Baldwin, Austen Chamberlain, Birkenhead, Churchill, MacDonald. Amongst my undergraduate contemporaries were Quentin Hogg, later Lord Hailsham; Randolph Churchill, in his youth a young man of seemingly unlimited promise never fulfilled; and John Boyd-Carpenter, a brilliant Union speaker. Occasionally a visiting sovereign such as the King of Greece or prominent literary figures such as Philip Guedalla and Salvador de Madariaga, would speak. Equally significant was the interest in religion in those years: the outstanding churchman, Dr William Temple, then Archbishop of York, came to Oxford in the summer of 1930 on what he described as a mission. For eight consecutive nights he preached to a packed congregation in St Mary's Church, relayed to an even larger overflow audience in the square outside. Those, for me, were the most fruitful, the most developing years in my life. Oxford became my spiritual home; it still is.

After coming down from Oxford, I began my legal studies. My mother said I must have a profession, and whether I continued it or not, the law would serve me well in politics. Once again she was right. Whilst still an undergraduate I had commenced eating the requisite number of Bar dinners at the Inner Temple. Even in those days to expect much for three shillings and sixpence was unreasonable, but the three course meal was horrible, and the wine barely drinkable. I was fortunate in finding a spacious flat in 19 Ennismore Gardens, SW7, facing that quiet and pretty square, and there I stayed until July 1934. Next door, as if a portent of the future, lived SM Bruce the Australian High Commissioner. The Bar vacations provided ample opportunities of acquiring a wider knowledge of Europe: France, Spain, Gibraltar, Italy, Austria, Hungary, Czechoslovakia and Germany were countries we visited. In the long vacation of 1933 I sailed to Nigeria for a month where my friend George Dalgleish had been posted in the British Colonial Service – an enlightening introduction to the problems of Africa. And during these Oxford and inner Temple years I began my collection of seventeenth and eighteenth century English furniture, as well as those pictures I could afford.

By mid-1934, having cleared the hurdles of Bar finals and thus qualified for admission to the English Bar, it seemed high time to settle in South Australia. I had not lived there since a child of nine. The prospect of a career in England, legal as well as political, looked alluring, but one could never ignore a sense of obligation to Australia where the family had prospered through numerous members of distinction since 1838. Meanwhile, during my brief visitation in 1931, I had fallen in love with a property near Bridgewater just placed upon the market. In February 1932 my attorneys purchased it for me from the executors of the late TC Wollaston for what nowadays looks like an incredibly small sum. (The world and Australia lay encompassed by the worst economic depression of the century.) Here was the site for my dream home which became *Arbury Park* named after *Arbury Hall*, the seat of our good friends Sir Francis and Lady Newdegate in Warwickshire who were so kind to me throughout my developing years. The year before my mother had recommended to me a leading Adelaide architect, Kenneth Milne, whom we met whilst in London. He was sympathetic to my Georgian taste and keen interest in architecture. This resulted in the beginning of *Arbury* in November 1934, and its virtual completion in August in 1935. This exercise occupied most of my inaugural period in South Australia; the association with Ken Milne proved of the happiest and most fruitful. My elderly relations shook greying heads at, in their eyes, such youthful extravagant folly, but in the end they were handsome enough to acclaim this lovely mid-eighteenth century style of English manor a triumph. Altogether it became my home for thirty years, where I carried my bride across the threshold in 1947, and where our four children spent their early lives. In those days surely no-one could have foreseen the cruel fate that led to its destruction as a country house by the Playford Government in 1964.

In May 1935, having resided in the State for the requisite time, the Supreme Court admitted me, on the basis of my English qualifications, to the South Australian Bar. Once settled in *Arbury*, I began to practise in Adelaide as a junior employee of the eminent legal firm Finlayson, Mayo, Astley & Hayward. The partners bearing those names were not only distinguished lawyers but exceedingly nice men. Ronald Finlayson, the most senior of them, understood my love of politics and my developing rural interests. He made no objection to absences entailed by the beginnings of political activities, nor to months away when embroiled in my first political skirmish for the newly created State seat of Onkaparinga in 1937. This looked like a Liberal stronghold; it had been part of a larger three-member constituency represented by HH Shannon, a seasoned politician eighteen years my senior. The real struggle lay in the party pre-selection, for whoever succeeded in the party endorsement would win the election. Shannon won, on a ration of five to four, but commentators thought my performance promising for the future. Looking back, my mistakes were awful, of the most elementary kind. It fell to the great Australian, Charles Hawker, later that year to teach me the art of electioneering when he took me for three weeks on his campaign in Wakefield for the Federal elections.

Gathering war clouds and no immediate political prospects, induced me to return to England and the Continent for most of 1938. My mother came with me, and despite international anxieties it was one of my happiest and most interesting years. Friends and contacts were helpful in Italy and France; in

London one met a variety of politicians, diplomats and business men. We made the first of what for me became several visits to Ulster to stay with Basil and Cynthia Brooke (later Lord and Lady Brookeborough) two of my greatest friends. London during the Munich crisis, though nerve-racking, was one of the dramatic experiences of my life. I thought then, as did the overwhelming majority of the British people, that Neville Chamberlain acted rightly in not going to war when he lacked the force necessary for success, and when public opinion was not geared up to a war complex. Forty years later my opinions are still unshaken: the intervening year made possible in September 1939 what could have proved disastrous in 1938.

My generation, nevertheless, like its predecessor, was doomed to fight. Australia, to its honour, declared war on Germany one hour after Chamberlain's historic statement to the House of Commons on 3 September 1939. For me, one course only seemed open – to join the army. At Geelong we had been given elementary tutelage in military training, little more than a parade ground drill, and dull it was. But knowing nothing about flying, and there being no opportunities in the navy, the alternatives appeared close. So as a first step I enlisted in the 13th Field Brigade, an artillery militia regiment, from which recruits to the 2nd AIF would be drawn. Lacking sufficient experience, I did not volunteer for the 6th and 7th Divisions which went to the Middle East, but waited for the formation of the 8th Division towards the end of 1940. We did initial training, as with the militia, at Woodside, and were then transferred to Puckapunyal. Of all my service experiences, those four months at Puckapunyal were almost the most hateful. Eventually we moved to Darwin, but after three days I was ordered to report to Adelaide for transfer to Headquarters RAA where I was supposed to do intelligence work. We sailed from Fremantle early in August 1941 in a 12,000 ton Dutch passenger ship, *Sibijak*. Accommodation for officers no doubt was uncomfortable, but conditions were appalling for us troops;

it was a relief to disembark in the sweltering heat of Singapore. Three weeks later I became attached to my new unit. But for me, there was virtually no intelligence work to do.

The story of the AIF in Malaya, as well as that of the four British Divisions, had been told oft-times. It is a depressing episode in British and Australian military history, culminating in our defeat by the Japanese at Singapore on 15 February 1942. I will not dwell upon those three and a half years in captivity. Of all the war books, the most descriptive on that subject is my friend Russell Braddon's best-seller *The Naked Island*, where our conditions and attitudes are accurately and vividly described. A little, however, I must add. Adversity, hardship, poverty, suffering and starvation are stern challenges to character. Until then I thought my education had occurred at Geelong and Oxford; an equally vital phase of it were those years in Changi. There most of us made some magnificent friendships; you beheld human nature at its loftiest and its lowest; you discovered the unfathomable, inner resources of the spirit; physically you realised how much more one can perform than ever seems possible in normal living. Those of us who had the good fortune of intellectual background fared best. There were always those reserves of mind to draw upon; it was possible to detach oneself from the slavery, the stink of latrines, the increasing debility of our appearance, the unending ration or rice, and escape to the world of higher reality. I was especially fortunate for much of those years in being detailed to give lectures on politics and history, to give personal tutorials to those wanting to learn and in assisting with the running of a camp library. These responsibilities occasioned mental activity, and the life I led provided resources to draw upon. The AIF camp command for three years endowed me with a sergeant's stripes in recognition of functions one tried to perform, but after release, and repatriation, the authorities at home refused to recognise any temporary promotions made during captivity.

So I entered the Army in 1939 as Gunner Downer and left

it on discharge on 15 November 1945 as Gunner Downer, a military career completely without distinction, but acquiring knowledge of my fellow men which proved the making of me as a politician.

~ 3 ~

The coming of peace ushered in a new era in world history, especially so it seemed to the millions who had been in the armed services. In many respects I was surprised how little conditions outwardly had changed. After being shut off from the world as prisoners-of-war, apart from the camp secret radio, I returned from captivity fearful that my mother, by that time seventy-four, had perished with anxiety, half expecting the substance of one's fortune destroyed and apprehensive of revolutionary alterations in the basis of Australian life. These were idle fears; no word can ever describe the joy of reunion with my mother and step-father, and my few surviving relatives, at the Adelaide railway station on 21 September 1945, nor of convalescent months during that spring and summer in the serenity and beauty of *Arbury*.

Signal events lay in store for the rest of the decade. In 1946 the Premier, Tom Playford, who amidst seething public controversy had just nationalised the Adelaide Electrical Supply Company, invited me to join the board of the South Australian Electricity Trust which he established in its place. As no political doors were opening, I accepted, although as I told the Premier, I could not distinguish a kilowatt from a kelvin; could not even mend a fuse. His reply was that I could bring a general view to bear on development problems, and in return gain valuable experience in an aspect of public administration. The latter certainly proved true. My three years on the Trust were interesting, educative, as well as congenial with four very diverse colleagues: HTM Angwin, the state Engineer-in-Chief chaired our deliberations; Sir Richard Butler, a former Premier was Deputy Chairman; the remaining two, FH Harrison and JW

Harrod, like Angwin, were engineers. Our principal tasks were to exploit the latent coal reserves at Leigh Creek; in conjunction with this to build a power station in the north of the State; to reticulate electricity more widely throughout rural area. All this the Trust accomplished. Leigh Creek open cut mining proceeded space; we selected a site in Spencer Gulf near Port Augusta for the power station; the country received electricity as never before.

The same year Playford, at the request of several members of the Art Gallery board, appointed me to that body. There I served for seventeen years, resigning at the end of 1963 only because of my transition to London as High Commissioner. Of all my public appointments, none has given me more pleasure. Sir Edward Morgan, a cultivated lawyer with admirable tests and knowledge of pictures, porcelain, and antique furniture was chairman, succeeded for a while by Sir Lloyd Dumas the notable journalist. Other colleagues were Sir Hans Heysen, Ivor Hele, John Goodchild and Lady Hayward. The two directors in these years were Louis McCubbin, and after his death, Robert Cambell. Very different in their methods, both made an immense contribution to the Gallery which has certainly not been equalled since.

It would be unjust and ungrateful not to acknowledge my gratitude to Sir Thomas Playford (as he became) for these two appointments. It is lamentable that as I progressed in national politics, our relations deteriorated, culminating in the crisis over *Arbury* early in 1964.

But 1946 brought a more profound event in my life than joining the electricity Trust and the Art Gallery. At a cocktail party at the South Australian Hotel in July, a friend – now Mr Justice Fisher of the Federal Court – introduced me to Mary Gosse. Instantaneously she seemed different from any girl I had ever met. We did not see one another again until October. Thereafter the pace quickened. At *Wairoa* on the night of 16 December, three days after her 22nd birthday, I asked her to marry me; to my delight she accepted. On 7 January 1947 we announced the glad tidings to the world. We chose St George's Day, Shakespeare's birthday, for our wedding day. And so on 23 April we were married in our parish church at Crafers by Aubrey Pain, one of the 8th Division padres, Tony Newsom, a magnificent Changi friend, acting as best man. Deliberately we ordained a quiet country wedding, with merely sixty-two close relations and real friends. Mary's parents, later to become Sir James and Lady Gosse, gave a charming reception at their Aldgate home *Wairoa*, without speeches except for a toast followed by a few words of thanksgiving from me. After two days at *Arbury* we travelled by train to Western Australia on our honeymoon, returning three weeks later by sea in the Shaw Savill liner *Corinthic* on her maiden voyage. And we lived happily ever after.

Good news flowed throughout 1948. On 28 January our eldest child was born, Stella Mary. By a pleasant coincidence she shared the same birthday as her distinguished great-uncle Alexander George Downer, the first Downer to be born in South Australia, 109 years before. Not long after, Mr Chifley, the Labor Prime Minister, announced the Government's plans to increase the size of the House of Representatives from seventy-four to one hundred and twenty-four seats, and the Senate from thirty-six to sixty. Out of the electoral melting-pot emerged the new rural constituency of Angas, stretching from the top of Mount Lofty to the Victorian border beyond Renmark, and to the north-east up to the New South Wales Frontier near Broken Hill. It was a vast area, but it included our own district, the Barossa country which my father had represented in the long ago, and much of Wakefield where Charles Hawker taught me political tactics. The pundits pronounced it a likely Liberal seat, estimating a majority of 3000. Playford told me he would not forsake State politics for a seat with only that margin. In any case, at last the long hoped for opportunity had come. Quickly I announced my candidature for Liberal pre-selection, to be followed by four others. Then began a strenuous campaign for party endorsement, not without some disagreeable features. The sitting MP for Barker, the highly respected, unconventional, controversial Archie Cameron (destined to be the next Speaker of the House) actively opposed me; reports came in that the Premier preferred one of his friends, a fruit grower, as did Cameron. In March 1949 the plebiscite was taken. Thanks to widespread support from my own area, the Onkaparinga Valley, much of the Barossa as well as Renmark and other Murray irrigation settlements, reinforced by help from the Burra and Peterborough districts, I secured an overall majority against the combined vote of my opponents. The Liberal endorsement accomplished, one proceeded hopefully to the general elections chosen by Chifley for 10 December 1949. They marked a watershed in Australian history. After eight years in office, the Labor party, which under Chifley had become increasingly socialistic, suffered a decisive defeat from which they never recovered until the close of 1972. Menzies, with his cohorts of young ex-servicemen, swept into office to begin his record-breaking prime ministership of sixteen years. In the Australian-wide Liberal swing my majority in Angas over the Labor candidate stood at nearly 10,500. Here, at last, as fulfilment of primary ambition. Yet I had taken a long time: I was thirty-nine.

Amidst so much campaigning, another event of family importance occurred. On 15 September our second child Angela was born in Adelaide. Three of our four children were born in election years; the youngest, Una, was conceived in another. Despite our increasing family, and their extreme youthfulness, Mary gave me unstinting support both in the constituency and in Canberra. Her easy manner, personal charm, ability to mix readily with every section of the community, assisted me, and the Liberal party, in ways which can never be sufficiently applauded. She also emerged as a frank and honest critic of my endeavours, a difficult but necessary role for a wife to play in the advancement of her husband's career. Twenty-five years later, she was to be acclaimed by a leading British Labor Cabinet Minister as the most outstanding diplomat's wife in London.

Parliament assembled on 22 February 1950. Mary and my mother attended for the great event. But I shall never forget the awesome coldness of the Chamber when an attendant showed us over it the afternoon before. How would one ever be able to speak in this place? Unlike most of the new MPs I avoided the *Address-in-Reply* debate, the customary forum for maiden speeches. After asking a few questions of ministers at Question Time, with trepidation, it seemed better to wait until the 21 March for the first foreign affairs debate, directing my speech to Japanese peace proposals and the future role Australia should play in East and South-East Asia. Thereafter, life as a parliamentarian grew easier, but it took me several years to feel at home in the House of Representatives, so much for a newcomer is there to learn. And nothing can so disadvantage a fledgling MP as to become a minister too soon.

This first of the seven Parliaments to which I belonged proved short and turbulent. War broke out in Korea; the Government decided to participate in a United Nations force. In Canberra, although commanding a large majority in the lower House, Labor still controlled the Senate. They used their advantage to block the Government's banking bills, believing that the Governor-general, McKell, as a previous Labor Premier of New South Wales, would never accede to Menzies' request for a double dissolution. In this they were wrong. With the two Houses deadlocked, Menzies advised the Governor-General that the constitutional requirements for a double dissolution could now apply. To the Labor party's chagrin McKell agreed, an action for which they never forgave him, as with another nominee of theirs, Sir John Kerr, twenty-four years later. So once again we cast our electoral bread upon the waters, and all of us younger men were up for election before we had time to settle properly into our seats. The results completely justified the Prime Minister's strategy. At the general elections on 26 April 1951, the Government secured a majority in both Houses. In Angas the Labor candidate was my sole opponent; after a friendly campaign my majority edged up to 11,000. Everyone felt we could now look forward to three years of political stability.

During this Parliament good fortune continued to favour me. On 9 September 1951, our son Alexander John Gosse was born in Adelaide amidst family rejoicings. In February 1952, the Government established a Joint Parliamentary Committee on Foreign Affairs to which the Liberal Parliamentary Party elected me. By that time Casey had become Foreign Minister, and the information, enlightenment, and encouragement he gave to us members made this a rewarding exercise. The year 1953, both then and in retrospect, seemed the happiest year of my life. George VI had died the previous year (we heard the news one evening amidst a parliamentary debate); the young Queen was to be crowned on 2 June. Every British Commonwealth Parliament had the right to send a delegation to the coronation, and as usual for our members, all parliamentary committees were selected by secret ballot of their respective parliamentary parties. Inevitably there was a big field of Liberal MPs, but only the principle of nothing ventured, nothing gained, I nominated. I could hardly believe my ears when told my name came out on top of the list, with FM Osborne and Dr Donald Cameron (subsequently both able Ministers) as colleagues. We sailed from Fremantle in the liner *Oronsay* (we were allowed to take our wives) on the 4 May with five State Premiers aboard, as well as delegates from the Opposition and Country parties. Disembarking at Naples, Mary and I proceeded to Rome for a brief visit, thence to London to prepare for the historic ceremonies. Official hospitality abounded; we were allotted seats in Westminster Abbey, invited to the splendours of a Buckingham Palace reception, the remarkable Commonwealth Parliamentary luncheon to the Queen and Prince Philip in Westminster Hall, followed by a multitude of other grand occasions. For Mary and me these were four months of intense delight. It was the first time we had been together in England and Europe. Later in the summer we visited friends in various parts of England, flew to Ulster to stay with Lord and Lady Brookeborough, then crossed to Holland, West Germany, Paris and Italy. There I introduced Mary to Bellagio on Lake Como where we were joined by Cynthia Brookeborough; thence the three of us continued to Venice, Ravenna, Florence and Rome. At Castel Gandolfo, Pope Pius XII granted us a private audience, one of the most uplifting spiritual experiences of our lives. Despite the magnetism of our three little children at home, and the prospect of seeing our mothers again, to say nothing of parliamentary duties, returning to Australia on 6 September was not unalloyed joy.

By the autumn of 1954 the triennial parliamentary term had expired. Elections took place on 29 May. To my relief and satisfaction I was returned for Angas unopposed, a circumstance which enabled me to support colleagues in other electorates. Once more the Government won with a substantial majority, and once again the auguries indicated three stable years ahead. But unforeseen events impelled the Prime Minister to act otherwise and in my personal life shadows began to fall. The New Year commenced ominously with the most terrible bushfires ever recorded in the Mount Lofty Ranges. *Marble Hill*, the Governor's official summer residence, perished in the flames; the Governor and Lady George escaped narrowly with their lives. Towards the end of March, my mother suffered a paralytic stroke. A cruel, debilitating decline followed, until finally the end came on 28 November in the cottage at *Arbury* where we brought her as soon as it had been remodelled for her occupation. To make matters words, D'Arcy Addison, my step-father, died suddenly, approaching eighty-three, three months before in Adelaide. I shall never be certain whether she comprehended the news I had to impart to her; intuitively – because she was in fact a mystic – perhaps she did. By one of life's dramatic coincidences, her funeral took place on the fifty-sixth anniversary of her marriage to my father – the 29 November. She lived until eighty-four and a half, a personality of high spirituality who never grew old until stricken eight months before. No son could have been blessed with a more loving, devoted, companionable mother, whose wisdom, tolerance, understanding, and advice were formative elements in my own mental development and any success I have been able to achieve.

My personal grief was not assuaged by political circumstances. As 1955 progressed, Australia became engrossed in a *cause célèbre* known as the 'Petrov Affair'. Dr Evatt, the Labor leader, adopted such a curious attitude to this case, giving the impression of sympathising with Soviet attitudes towards the defector from the Russian diplomatic service. Moreover, the Labor party by now had developed what proved a fatal split largely on a sectarian basis on the issue of Communism, highlighted by Evatt's apparent leanings towards the Left. Seizing on these divisions, coupled with mounting dissatisfaction with Evatt's leadership, Menzies decided to seek a premature dissolution of the House of Representatives. Polling took place on 10 December, a lucky date in the Liberal calendar; once again the Government triumphed. Unlike 1954, this time I had Labor and Independent candidates to contend with. But my constituents were more generous than ever: my majority over both opponents exceeded 12,000 and over Labor 13,000. The campaign for me throughout had been clouded by misery and gloom on account of my mother, and I was determined to take my family abroad for a change of scene. So early in January, with the three children (and a fourth on the way) we sailed for Ceylon in the Himalaya, returning six weeks later for the opening of the new Parliament on 14 February.

I shall ever be grateful to Ceylon, and the P & O liners we sailed in, for the balm they provided after the sorrows of 1955.

The Australian High Commissioner, Mr Peachy, showed all of us much kindness. He arranged an interview with the vigorous, unconventional Prime Minister Sir John Kotelawala, ('I keep two houses, one for habitations, the other for cohabitation'), and various officials. Whilst at Nuwara Eliya we were entertained at luncheon by a Ceylonese MP over the hottest curry in my experience. The Colombo press also seemed interested in Australian-Ceylon relations.

Happier portents now lay ahead. On 15 March our fourth child was born in Adelaide. We called her Una Joanna after her two grandmothers; she was christened in November by the Bishop of Adelaide in the Arbury chapel on its completion as a memorial to my mother.

In 1956 the Cabinet dedicated to set up a Joint Parliamentary Committee on the Constitution, and on this I won a place. Its deliberations between 1956 until I became a minister in March 1958 were amongst the most interesting things in my career. The object of our researches lay in discovering what unity the three parties could achieve towards constitutional reform in the light of more than half a century of experience and future needs could achieve towards constitutional reform in the light of more than half a century of experience and future needs. The Opposition fielded a strong team: Calwell (then Deputy Leader), Whitlam, Ward, Pollard, McKenna (their leader in the Senate) and Kennelly, also a senator. Sir Neil O'Sullivan, the Attorney-General, led the Liberals, with Percy Joske QC, Senator Wright, an able though contentious Tasmanian lawyer, and myself; the Country Party nominated Hamilton from Western Australia, and David Drummond from New South Wales. The Committee travelled in all States, taking evidence from many sources, besides frequent sittings in Canberra. Of immense assistance was John Richardson, now a law professor, then a law officer in the Attorney-General's department. O'Sullivan optimistically dubbed him the young Garran. After a few months we all became friends. Discussions were forthright, unreserved and constructive. Party divisions, though never far away, subsided. We grew to tolerate each other's approaches not merely to constitutional problems but to the broader spectrum of politics. Firebrands in the House such as Eddie Ward appeared in a new light sitting around conference table away from the searchlights of press and television. He and I though philosophically poles apart, developed a genuine regard for each other; even closer were my relations with Calwell and Whitlam. As a by-product of those years I became convinced of the tremendous value of joint parliamentary committees. They educate both sides of politics to a comprehension of one another's attitudes – and problems; they generate tolerance, remove bitterness. When such associations blossom into friendship, acerbities soften in public debates, and the legislative process is enhanced.

The Committee reported to Parliament in two stages: an interim report on 1 October 1958, and a final report on 25 November 1959. Our proposals were too radical for Menzies and Berwick who by then had succeeded O'Sullivan as Attorney-General. Many Liberal and Country party senators were shocked by our plan for simultaneous elections for the Senate and House of Representatives, which they regarded as a diminution of the power and authority of the Upper House. We had to wait until 1977 for a Liberal-Country administration to endorse this amendment in a referendum. Alas! Though attracting over sixty per cent of total votes cast, it failed to carry a majority of the States. Many years will pass before this practical, realistic, economical reform will become enshrined in the Constitution.

By the beginning of 1958, we arranged to make a short visit to England and the Continent during the winter recess. The stars ordained otherwise. Towards the end of February, the Prime Minister summoned me to his room, opening the discussion with the words, 'Alick, I want to discuss your future.' He proposed to make me a minister; he could not then say what portfolio, though I expressed a preference for Immigration. The announcement would not be made until next month. 'Meanwhile,' and he glared at me, 'you will tell no one.' But of course within ten minutes I had imparted these tremendous tidings to the most discreet of all persons, Mary. And so on 20 March 1958 I was sworn in at Admiralty House, Sydney, by Field Marshal Sir William Slim, as Minister for Immigration.

The Ministry at that time comprised twenty-one members, the senior twelve constituting the Cabinet. Being the new boy my place was bottom of the list. My immediate predecessor, Athol Townley, sat in Cabinet, so in that respect my department suffered temporary disadvantage. From the start limitless help was proffered by THE Heyes (later Sir Tasman) the permanent head and senior officers. Heyes combined untiring energy with tact and experience. Calwell had appointed him Secretary of the department after its inauguration in 1945, so by 1958 no man in Australia knew so much about immigration in its national and international ramifications as this distinguished civil servant. I had known him a little before; a few weeks prior to my elevation he told my unbelieving ears I would be his new minister. From the moment his prophecy was fulfilled we established a close rapport. Heyes possessed an uncanny flair for politics in the wider sense: he displayed no party alignment, acted impeccably both to Government and Opposition members alike, but he understood politicians, their motives, their ambitions, just as he accurately assessed the qualities of his fellow departmental heads. During those months of my novitiate he guided me through labyrinthic minefields of ministerial colleagues who might be jealous or touchy, Labor leaders who could prove difficult, union bosses, controversial ecclesiastics, journalists – in short, the whole range of those concerned with nation-building. Never presuming to impinge on the Minister's authority, his attitude towards me resembled a benign uncle, a real friend. No words can express adequately my appreciation of his assistance until his retirement in 1961.

Moreover, Sir Tasman co-operated enthusiastically and skilfully in the fulfilment of my own ideas. It seemed wise, as well as opportune, to place more emphasis on immigration from Britain, not only on ethnic grounds but to counter criticisms that Australia had been attracting too many southern Europeans. Accordingly, we extended my predecessor's 'Bring Out a Briton' campaign to include all personal dependants under nineteen years old. This, in fact, was one of the most glittering travel bargains of all time, for it meant that a man, his wife and any number of children under nineteen could emigrate from Britain to Australia for merely £20. Furthermore, my knowledge of British conditions led me to decentralise our recruiting processes from London. By the middle of 1958 I had secured the concurrence of my friend Lord Brookeborough, the Ulster Prime Minister, to open an Australian immigration office in Belfast. Simultaneously, we established centres in Edinburgh and Manchester, with the promise of more to follow if these plans succeeded. Eventually, immigration offices in conjunction with the Trade Department were set up in Birmingham, Leeds, Cardiff, Newcastle-upon-Tyne, with a smaller office in Glasgow. Foolishly, most of these centres were closed between 1972 and 1975, consequent upon the Whitlam administration's sharp reduction of our immigrant intake; by 1978 only Edinburgh and Manchester remained.

Immediately on becoming Minister, a formidable task faced me. During Townley's relatively brief period at Immigration, the Cabinet had decided on a thoroughgoing overhaul of immigration legislation since Federation, together with revision of the nationality acts. I asked for time to consider these bills, as well as to make some proposals of my own. The result was the Migration Act which I presented to the House of May Day 1958. Apart from consolidating numerous statutes, its main features were the abolition of the dictation test, a harsh practice of excluding intending settlers dating from 1901, which had rightly attracted widespread international criticism. In its stead we substituted a system of entry permits; revocation of the Minster's power to order deportation of migrants who had committed no crime within five years of their arrival except on the recommendation of an independent legal commissioner; prohibition of children being taken out of the country in cases of disputed custody unless by consent of both parents or a court; officers engaged in searching for prohibited immigrants or deportees or documents related to them must have search warrants; establishment of detention centres for deportees who were not criminals pending deportation, instead of casting them into prisons. This last was my own doing, and evoked a very favourable response. The Bill received a warm press and eventually to my relief passed through Parliament without difficulty, thanks to our own rank and file members and helpful co-operation from Percy Clarey who led the debates for Labor.

Our next reformist legislation swept away discrimination against naturalised settlers, placing them on the same footing as native Australians except when naturalisation had been obtained by fraud. I introduced these amendments to the Nationality Act on 26th August, stating that henceforth there would be no first of second class citizenship: in future Australian citizenship would be a one class train. These proposals also achieved an easy passage.

Concentration on British migration did not involve neglect of our valuable inflow from Europe. In August 1958 I renewed with five years. At a ceremony at Port Melbourne in November I welcomed the 100,000th Dutch migrant to Australia since 1946. This was a period when splendid people from north-western Europe flocked to Australia. In a planned target of 115,000 settlers for 1958-59 we provided for over 10,000 Dutch, 5000 Germans, 2500 Austrians, 2000 Danes, 1500 from Scandinavia and Switzerland, 59,000 from Britain and Eire, between 8000 and 9000 refugees, many of whom came from iron curtain countries. From the Mediterranean we promised 16,000 Italians, 7000 Greeks, 1000 Maltese. How different the story is twenty years later!

By November it was election time again. Polling took place on 22 November, with another substantial victory. Menzies recast the Ministry, adding a twenty-second minister. Both Sir Arthur Fadden and Sir Philip McBride retired from Parliament and the Cabinet, as did O'Sullivan (though not from the Senate) Holt became Treasurer, Sir Garfield Barwick Attorney-General, McMahon Minister for Labor. To my delight the Prime Minister leapfrogged me from twenty-first place to eleventh, with a seat in the Cabinet. Immigration remained my responsibility, to which he added early in 1959 the interesting task of being assistant to the Prime Minister in his departmental work. We were sworn in by Sir William Slim in Canberra on 10 December.

The year 1959 proved a fascinating and constructive year. Between mid-May and mid-July I made my first international migration mission. With Mary, our three elder children accompanied us; officials consisted of Sir Tasman Heyes, helped by ever-resourceful, effervescent Lady Heyes, Edward Waterman, a brilliant public relations officer, and John Goodwin my private secretary. Air travel by Constellation was slower in those days but comfortable. Altogether our journey took us to nine countries, starting with Athens for talks with Greek ministers, then to Rome where we were warmly received. The conversations with Signor Pella, the Foreign Minister, were in French, but other Italian ministers and civil servant we dealt with negotiated in English.

One morning Pope John XXIII graciously granted us a private audience at the Vatican. The old man's charm was infectious, as also his sense of humour. He knew no English, so we spoke alternating between my very limited Italian and French. He exuded kindliness towards our children – who looked overawed by the encounter – stroking Angela's hair and saying his name was Angelo. He complained of his restricted life now that he was Pope, describing himself, '*Je suis prisonnier de luxe*.' No wonder he became so widely beloved.

After a brief stop in Milan, where we had opened a subsidiary immigration office, I took the next five days off introducing our young to the ineffable delights of Venice and Baveno on Lake Maggiore. From there we caught the *Simplon Express*, by then shabbily in decline, to Paris. My Department and I were keen to discover whether opportunities existed for attracting French settlers; useful discussions ensued preparatory to opening an Australian immigration office in Paris. And so across to London by the night ferry late in May. The Hyde Park Hotel gave us a spacious flat mostly overlooking the park, and this remained our headquarters for three weeks.

In Britain there was much to do. Publicity is essential for any migration programme, and here, as elsewhere, the press assisted generously thanks to Waterman's untiring groundwork. One of my themes was the imbalance of the sexes at home; Australia needed more single women for men to marry, and this of course, is just the sort of story newspapers headline. Heyes talked to senior officials in the Commonwealth and Home offices; I met various ministers and MPs including the Commonwealth Secretary Lord Home, an association later to blossom into friendship, and Alport the Minister of State in the House of Commons who seemed stuffy and reserved. My all too brief encounter with Harold Macmillan, the Prime Minister, at 10 Downing Street, caught him in an unfavourable moment, but during my subsequent visit three years later he revealed more of his affability and aplomb. In London I announced a further bait to British nationals called by the Department 'Nest Egg'. This extended the £10 a head assisted passage privilege to married couples who could bring £500 to Australia. No nomination was required; provided they could fulfil usual immigration standards we would welcome them on these very favourable terms.

I was anxious to inspect the provincial offices opened

the previous year, so we paid a fleeting visit to Edinburgh, and a longer one to Northern Ireland where we divided our time between a happy weekend with the Brookeboroughs at Colebrook and official duties in Belfast. Mistakenly I omitted Manchester, but Heyes and Waterman spent a useful day there.

Holland was our next country. Sir Edwin McCarthy, the Australian Ambassador, kindly invited us to stay at the embassy; the Dutch, on their part, were still interested in emigration to Australia, and our migration office in The Hague thrived. I made a speech in the Rosenzal, in the picturesque Parliament buildings, the Government gave us a spectacular banquet in a lovely medieval castle, *Muiderslot*, and in other aspects displayed friendliness, appreciation, and hospitality. Newspapers in Amsterdam and The Hague prominently featured our presence. All in all, these were a useful three days.

From The Hague the flight is short to Copenhagen. Australia has long valued her Danish settlers; Heyes was keen that I should see our activities there, and meet Danish officials. Copenhagen is always pleasurable; the rather overpowering royal suite according us at the Hotel Angleterre did not detract from diplomacy. A night train then took us to Cologne, the centre of our German activities. We stayed at the Dom Hotel, opposite what to me is one of Europe's most exalting cathedrals: I instructed my officials to enter it every morning before setting out on our crowded programme. This was one of my decrees which they probably never observed in the manner the Minister intended!

German immigration to Australia dates back to the close of the 1830s, and this historical background should enable any itinerant Australian Minister to play down the scars left by two world wars. For 1959-1960 we planned to achieve 11,000 German settlers, but prosperity in West Germany made suitable people harder to attract, nor did the German Government smile on our activities. However, the attitude of ministers and officials was cordial; they appeared pleased by some concessions I announced, and their hospitality at a magnificent dinner in the Petersburg, and elegant hotel (now closed) on one of the peaks of the Seven Mountains overlooking the Rhine, was superb. At the instigation of our imaginative chief migration officer, Denis Winterbottom, we continued by car our progress to Austria along the celebrated Romantische Strasse, spending a night in an ancient inn at Dinkelsbuhl, during which a drunken porter burst into our bedroom where Alexander was also sleeping, making off with his underclothes. This enchanting drive ended at Salzburg, in itself the culmination of alpine beauty. From there the train took us to Vienna.

Australia's activities in Austria were handicapped by the refusal of our Foreign Ministry to establish reciprocal diplomatic relations. The Government manifested their resentment by taking no notice of my visit, nor proffering entertainment of any sort. Nevertheless leading ministers were prepared to receive me. Thus I paid very pleasant calls on Dr Bruno Kreisky, the Foreign minister, a highly intelligent, likeable Jew, who eventually graduated to Chancellor. The Vice-Chancellor, Dr Pitterman, was equally agreeable, likewise Herr Helmer the Minister for the Interior. I had no difficulty in expressing personal regrets at our lack of diplomatic representation: considering Austria's central position, its proximity to iron curtain countries, our intake of refugees, added to the fact that we maintained immigration offices in Linz and Vienna, the absence of an embassy seemed parsimonious folly. Australia's formal relations were handled by the British Ambassador who was then Sir James Bowker, a charming man with an animated, outgoing Lebanese wife. Both were kindness itself during out stay. A friendly Viennese press advertised my visit, gave favourable reportage to my undertaking to accept more refugees, as well as my plea for more Austrian migrants. Despite the embarrassment mentioned, one departed – always reluctantly leaving Austria – feeling that goodwill had been accomplished.

The time had now come to return home. With trepidation

we all embarked on a Britannia aircraft at Zurich, for a severe electrical storm menaced us from all sides. After take off we endured a frightening hour, but Melbourne, our destination, lay safely ahead. The Department issued an excellent statement summarising the results of this two months' mission to coincide with our arrival. I also said that if the Government wished, we could successfully increase next year's target to 125,000. As it was, we had exceeded the 1958-1959 aim by nearly 2000, to give us just short of 117,000 for that financial year.

Our hopes for 1959-1960 proved conservative. The result showed 133,684, highly satisfactory considering swelling prosperity in Europe. More than half came from the United Kingdom whose economy Macmillan summarised in his election slogan, 'You've never had it so good.' But despite these successes, a section of the press fanned a campaign for an annual quota of Asians. Newspapers such as the *Melbourne Herald* and those controlled by Rupert Murdoch constantly criticised my refusal – with strong Cabinet concurrence – to countenance such a doubtful expedient. In July 1960, in my Roy Milne Memorial lecture in Sydney, entitled *The Influence of Migration of Australian Foreign Policy*, I attempted some long-range thinking on the consequences of our program, and its inevitable dilution of the historical Anglo-Australian relationship. My officers disagreed, with profound unease, when I showed them the script, but I persisted; and the extraordinarily full and favourable press reportage, followed by praising leading articles, justified my primary intention of stimulating public discussion on where Australia was heading. This was a period when I tried to project people's minds into the opening decade of the twenty-first century. Repeatedly, I urged an objective of a thirty million population between 2000 and 2010. My views are still unchanged; it is tragic that pusillanimous policies in the 1970s rendered this virtually impossible.

By 1961 Australia struck an economic rainstorm. For me it was a contentious year. Business confidence declined;

unemployment rose towards 114,000 or nearly three precent of the workforce. These were high figures after the prosperity of the 1950s, although in the late 1970s they would have seemed miraculously low. Unskilled migrants bore the brunt of the recession. To demonstrate their dissatisfaction a small militant minority inflamed a riot in July at Bonegilla, then our principal holding centre. The press naturally made vivid play of these events, with opponents of immigration demanding curtailment of the programme. This we declined to do; instead we decided promptly to suspend temporarily the inflow of unskilled workers, whilst maintaining the overall target of 125,000.

About this time a departmental problem arose as to who would succeed Sir Tasman Heyes as Secretary when he retired in November. Few people lamented his reaching the retiring age more than me. No one of comparable stature existed amongst his subordinates, although the standard of senior officers was high. Amongst the various contenders Mr Peter (later Sir Peter) Heydon, deputy secretary of External Affairs, seemed the most promising. Menzies thought well of him, a factor which ensured his appointment when I placed the nomination before Cabinet.

Other shadows appeared. I used to liken the Immigration portfolio to a kettle on a hot stove, seldom far from coming to the boil. Throughout my nearly six years administration of this department a series of disputed cases involved me in the nation-wide controversies, sometimes promoted by the pro-Asian section of the press (the *Melbourne Herald* and Packer of the *Sydney Daily Telegraph* became principal critics), sometimes at the instance of the Labor party for political purposes. We were now heading towards an election in the most awkward economic circumstances since Menzies' advent to power in 1949. Calwell led the Opposition, with Whitlam – whom he never liked nor trusted – as his deputy. It so happened that in September the worst of my *causes célèbres* blew up without warning. The Adelaide University had appointed a German-Israeli lecturer, YS Brenner, to a teaching post. On applying for an entry permit, our security service (ASIO) placed before my department one of the strongest, and best substantiated, objection I had seen. It seemed wrong to admit to a position of influence over a young man with such an adverse record. Accordingly I refuse him entry. All hell broke loose. Labor MPs such as Cairns, Clyde Cameron, Allan Fraser, Gordon Bryant and Whitlam in part, seized the opportunity to attack the Government. They received plenty of support from left-wing academics; the popular press (as distinct from most of the leading morning newspapers) screamed abuse of me. Throughout October the battle raged, with spirited scenes in Parliament. But I remained adamant. The Cabinet and all Liberal and Country party members backed me, including the youthful backbencher Malcolm Fraser in a long, well-reasoned speech to his electorate. Brenner never came. Throughout the ensuing election campaign, reverberations of this thunderstorm sounded in all States, most notably in a demonstration against the Prime Minister at his Hobart meeting.

The December poll brought us, as a Government, to the precipice of defeat. After prolonged doubt, we emerged with a majority of two. Two valuable colleagues and friends, Dr Cameron the Health Minister and FM Osborne, the Repatriation Minister, lost their seats. For us survivors all our previous votes slumped sharply. In Angas, the figures were the worst in my seven elections, with a majority over Labor fallen to little more than 8000. Economic decline was the principal cause; another lay in our not being sufficiently in contact with industry and business. Many customary Liberal voters, including one of my brothers-in-law, deserted us on this occasion. The Prime Minister made as few changes as possible in the administration; my place in the Cabinet hierarchy advanced to tenth, with Sir Garfield Barwick the new foreign Minister and Charles Adermann, Minister for Primary Industry, ranking below me.

The opening months of 1962 were stormy. With a floor

majority of one (after having provided the Speaker, Sir John McLeay) the Opposition naturally beset us with whatever difficulties they could conjure. Hostility smouldered from most of the Sydney press. The *Sydney Morning Herald*, antagonistic to Menzies, had backed Calwell in the elections; the Murdoch newspapers were also against us. In Canberra the parliamentary parties remained loyal, except for manoeuvres on occasions by the disgruntled. One of these affected me. The anti-communist obsession of WC Wentworth and Sir Wilfred Kent-Hughes (the latter a dispossessed minister who had fallen foul of Menzies) objected to my deportation of an illegal Chinese immigrant, Willie Wong. They believed his repatriation to China would result in his execution. Through their use of the press, a nation-wide controversy ensued. They went so far as to threaten the Government with defeat of the adjournment of the House unless my department took some countervailing measures. After an urgent plea by Holt as deputy Liberal leader (the Prime Minister was away) I cabled the ship's captain to hold Wong in Hong Kong pending further investigation. This prevarication saved the Government from defeat, but the message arrived too late. Willie Wong had crossed into China. I do not believe for one moment he lost his life.

Simultaneously, other controversies in Parliament and the press erupted concerning two Malay pearl divers in Darwin, also illegal immigrants, and three deserters from a Portuguese man-of-war. From the start I wanted to grant the Portuguese asylum, but felt the Malays should return home to their families. The Foreign Affairs department thought otherwise, fearing damage to our relations with Malaya if the pearlers were deported; on the other hand they did not wish to risk offending the government of Portugal. Barwick and I compromised by permitting all to remain in Australia, for which we reaped commendation by our critics.

The economic clouds through which we were passing aroused anxiety as to whether they would receive the 125,000 settlers provided for in the Budget. The Labor party seized on our restriction of unskilled workers as evidence of the Government's alleged financial mismanagement. Looking back, it is illuminating to observe the intense support of the immigration programme in the 1950s and 1960s as compared with the lukewarm attitude displayed in the 1970s. But now, in my personal life, a far more worrying shadow loomed: the determination of the South Australian Cabinet to build their projected south-eastern freeway right through the centre of *Arbury Park*. The controversy flared into excitable newspaper headlines, according much support to me and my family. Already the doom of *Arbury* as a private country house became apparent.

By May the sun shone again. Earlier I had secured Menzies' concurrence to undertake another international migration mission. He would only grant me six weeks ('My boy, I am allergic to travel') so perforce arrangements were more crowded than in 1959. Mary gave me immense assistance. I also took Peter Heydon as head of my department, and Jeffrey Champion my private secretary. It was a smaller entourage than before, but we accomplished much. Departing from Sydney on 22 May, we flew to New York where Roden Cutler, later Governor of New South Wales, was Consul-General; then to Washington for talks with American officials, not on immigration policies (apart from refugees from China) but primarily to brief myself as a cabinet minister on American thinking on world problems. We stayed at the Australian Embassy with Sir Howard Beale, our Ambassador, who gave me considerable help. One morning he took me to the White House to meet President Kennedy. His charm, boyishness and ease of manner are unforgettable. Looking younger, and more relaxed than in his photographs, he seemed interested in Australia, manifested a cordial relationship with Beale – to the Ambassador's credit.

Then followed from New York a night flight to London, and the inevitable press conference the next day. I divided my British visit into two sections – an initial three days at the end of May, and a further nine days after a Continental tour. On 29 May I signed with Duncan Sandys, the Commonwealth Secretary, a renewal of the British-Australian migration agreement for five years. Next morning the Queen received me at Buckingham Palace. The audience lasted for half an hour; she was so gracious, beautiful and easy to talk to that when I took my leave I could not help saying, 'Ma'am, if I may say so, you look absolutely marvellous!' She seemed a little surprised – Lord Carrington said English ministers customarily do not speak to the Queen in this way – but two of the courtiers quickly assuaged my fear of having gone too far. Long live the freer Australian idiom!

Our European tour commenced in Germany on 31 May. In Cologne a large Australian migration office had long flourished, but most of my activities took place in Bonn. As before, the German ministers and senior civil servants were friendly and hospitable. We agreed on renewing our migration agreement after it expired in August, but full employment in Germany, rising prosperity, presaged declining numbers of German settlers to Australia. I tried to counter these obstacles by urging the authorities, and the press, to take a long-term view of an emergent Australia, and the practical advantages to them of being on the historic migration links, dating back to the 1930s, between our two countries. And once again I asked, as elsewhere, for more single women. This, as one intended, appealed to the press who dubbed me an 'international skirt-chaser'.

Excellent as the German press coverage proved, it paled before the unexpectedly warm reception of the French. By 1962 we had opened an immigration office in central Paris: I believed the effort worthwhile to seek to persuade these notoriously non-migratory people of the advantages of life in Australia. Sir Ronald Walker, our Ambassador, gave me much assistance, accompanying me on my call on Monsieur Grandval, the Minister for Labor, who listened to me with exquisite politeness. Next followed a press conference at the embassy, and then, without warning, a television broadcast and a broadcast on *Radio Luxembourg.* The last two I had to do in French, doubtless breaking many grammatical rules, but the effect was electric. For days afterwards the embassy deluged with telephone calls, written enquiries from prospective settlers, whilst Paris newspapers, giving rise to amusing cartoons and friendly comment.

Warmed by these plaudits, we moved on in one of those splendid TEE trains to The Hague. Walter Crocker commanded the Australian embassy then, and a more distinguished Ambassador in the traditional mould it would be hard to find. The Dutch, as before, were hospitable and pleasant, except for a spirited talk one morning with Dr Luns, their talented Foreign minister. Luns expressed himself in forthright terms on Australian attitudes to Dutch New guinea, declaring that we were betraying a friendship in not supporting them against Indonesian claims. Privately I sympathised with his indignation, but defended our policy on grounds of future realism. The Prime Minister, Professor de Quay, showed no animosity in my conference with him, whilst the talks with Dr Beldam, Minister for Social Affairs, with responsibility for emigration, proceeded harmoniously enough. But the highlight of this visit was an audience of Queen Juliana at *Soestdijk. Soestdijk* is more a country house than a palace, conducted with a minimum of formality. The Queen received me in a small sitting-room upstairs, speaking fluent English. Our conversation covered a wide field: Dutch immigrants in Australia, the more liberal policies towards Asians which she believed in, religion, philosophy. After an hour and a half she asked whether I could stay to lunch; unfortunately I had to excuse myself on account of the afternoon's engagements. She radiated idealism, sympathy, quiet charm, a motherly femininity, all of which made her seem in my eyes a delightful personality.

From Amsterdam we took an uncomfortable night-train to Geneva where we stayed two days for discussion with the United Nations High Commissioner for Refugees, Dr Felix

Schnyder, and an old friend of Dutch emigration to Australia, Dr Haveman, then Director of that highly successful post-war body, the Intergovernmental Committee for European Migration (ICEM). Ever since 1946, Australia's acceptance of refugees has been praiseworthy, if not altogether altruistic. Thousands of these unfortunate people have benefited us greatly by their skills and culture, contributing richly to our national development. By 1962 we had received 260,000 refugees; I assured Dr Schnyder we would continue this policy. Geneva lies between the Jur and the Alps; the Simplon line to Milan passes Lake Maggiore, so the magnetism of two nights at Stress was irresistible. Refreshed by this aesthetic interlude, we arrived in Rome for negotiations we knew we would be difficult.

The Italian Government for the past year had shown concern over delays Italian migrants had encountered in finding speedy employment after landing in Australia. They demanded guarantee of jobs for their nationals which we were unable to give. Consequently, the official atmosphere in Rome was cool compared with 1959. Moreover, in dealing with Signor Lupis, the Under Secretary for Foreign Affairs, I encountered what Americans would call a 'tough cookie'. Lupis came from Sicily; he resented our preference for people from northern and central Italy. He knew no English, nor French, so we used an interpreter as my Italian was not sufficiently fluent to conduct intricate exchanged. In appearance he was the ugliest man I have ever seen, but his manners, though anything but polished, were formally correct. Eventually he agreed to renew the existing migration agreement for six months only and staged a publicised ceremony in the new Foreign Office for this purpose. Nevertheless, if the Government was cool, the newspapers were friendly. The results of my press conference and radio broadcast at The Hassler – one of my favourite hotels in the world – were widespread. Once again I pleaded not merely for skilled workers but for more single women to redress the imbalance of the sexes at home; once more the headlines followed in

Rome, and cities as diverse as Milan, Turin, Vienna, Messina. Conversations with other ministers, such as the Minister for Commerce, on the Common Market, were displeased by the big press coverage accorded my statements, particularly those directed towards Italian girls. Their Latin minds suspected sinister sexual motives. Apparently, the Vatican shared none of those complexes: Pope John, as three years before, received us – this time in his library - with informality, warmth, and charm, granting an audience of half and hour. On this occasion he presented me with a Papal medal and Mary with a rosary.

Our last European country was Spain. For some time my department and I had perceived advantages in endeavouring to attract Spanish migrants. So to Madrid I went, intent on gaining cooperation from the Spanish Government. This involved opening up a migration office, but as with Austria in 1959 the matter was complicated by our having no diplomatic representation in Madrid. Australian affairs were handled by the British, whose Ambassador, Sir George Labouchere, showed me much consideration. The ultimate hurdle, of course, lay in convincing General Franco of the rightness of our cause, for without his concurrence no emigration would be possible. The Gaudillo agreed to receive Haydon and me at *El Pardo*, his palace thirty miles outside Madrid. Its formality was startling. We were expected to wear full morning dress; the salons and corridors swarmed with elaborately dressed flunkeys. Eventually, after waiting one hour we were ushered into the presence. Franco, attired in a white uniform (it was summer, and hot) sat seated at a desk in a comparatively small room, untidy, littered with piles of documents and papers. A crucifix hung behind his chair. He greeted us civilly, but stiffly without a smile. The senior official from the Foreign Office who accompanied us acted as interpreter: Franco knew no English. As the conversation began I noticed with surprise a battery of television lights playing upon us from a corner of the room, supported by several press reporters. All this seemed such a contrast with the forbidding formality outside. Franco listened intently to my plea for his acceptance of a limited form of Spanish migration, showing neither dissent nor enthusiasm. Even in 1962 he seemed an old man, with much of the fire gone out. The fifth head of state who had received me on this tour, he was far and away the most rigid, the most remote.

Nevertheless, we achieved our aims. After some haggling over diplomatic representation, the Spaniards agreed to accept our Chief Migration Officer as Consul-General until such times as an Ambassador was accredited. All the officials we encountered exuded warmth and hospitality. Not only in Madrid but in Toledo we were royally entertained. We were shown the splendours of the Escorial, and the awe-inspiring monument to the victims of the Civil War, the Valley of the Fallen. Regrettably, my official duties prevented my seeing the Prado despite its proximity to the Ritz Hotel where we stayed, except in a most fleeting, unsatisfying way.

By 22 June we were back in London, but only until the next day when we flew to Northern Ireland. After staying the weekend at Colebrooke with the Prime Minister and Lady Brookeborough, I inspected our Belfast office as well as meeting various members of the Ulster administration. Later that week Duncan Sandys and the Duke of Devonshire, Minister of State at the Commonwealth Office, gave us a luncheon on behalf of the British Government at Marlborough House in the stately chandelier room. Sir Eric Harrison, the High Commissioner, was equally kind. Harold Macmillan, the Prime Minister, received me – this time most pleasantly – in his room at the House of Commons. Peter Carrington, always stimulating, amusing and hospitable, flourished as First Lord of the Admiralty.

Other useful occasions followed. A long talk at the Treasury with Selwyn Lloyd, Chancellor of the Exchequer, produced valuable information on some of Britain's financial problems. On that sunny June morning, speaking with confidence and assurance, I do not believe he had an inkling of the prime ministerial wrath to come the following month, when Macmillan, with a ruthlessness unprecedented in British politics this century, dramatically sacked seven of his ministers, including Selwyn Lloyd and Lord Kilmuir, the Lord Chancellor. Selwyn's friendly, forthcoming attitude contrasted vividly with that of the Home Secretary, RA (Rab) Butler. By virtue of his position, Butler in a sense was my opposite number, as the Home Office controls immigration to Britain. He received me with unexpected coldness and ill-manners which were repellent. Boredom seemed his only response to messages I conveyed from his friends Menzies, Casey and Brookeborough. As I entered his room, without rising from his chair or asking me to sit down, he began to defend immigration restrictions his Government had proclaimed not long before. Our exchanges were so formal, so unsatisfying, that I brought the interview to a close after barely fifteen minutes on the pretext of not occupying his time (I felt I was wasting my own). Very different was the demeanour of his assistant minister, Sir David Renton, the Minister of State, on whom I called immediately afterwards. Renton is a charming, relaxed man full of tolerance and understanding; we shared an excellent to and fro of ideas in a way that Butler made impossible. Renton, as with Selwyn Lloyd, fell from grace a few weeks later in Macmillan's violent purge. He did not hold office again. Yet it is only fair to add a postscript to the events of that morning. After I became High Commissioner, Butler's frigidity softened, and on my part I came to understand his brilliant, complex, honourable character. Having sat next to him at a Royal Academy banquet in the later 1960s, we walked out of the gallery arm-in-arm: thenceforth something approaching a friendship developed, which continues to exist.

By now my time limit had expired: we flew direct to Sydney, arriving on 2 July.

These efforts brought a rich harvest. Immigration for 1962–1963 showed a surplus of over 12,000 swelling the yearly arrivals to more than 137,000. An upsurge arose in British applications. The single girls started to arrive from most countries, including France. For the following year we felt able to predicate a target of 135,000. By the spring the economy was flourishing again. The numbers problem for the next few years disappeared.

Springtime also saw a revival of the Government's fortunes. The Prime Minister, with his customary sagacity, scented the opportunity of ridding himself of the parliamentary embarrassment of a majority of one. Early in October he told Cabinet ministers informally of his desire for a November election, a year before it was due. My New South Wales and Victorian colleagues showed enthusiasm for the idea; personally I felt hesitant, a reserve also shared by that likeable Tasmanian, Athol Townley. Menzies brushed aside any objections I offered, and events proved him triumphantly right. To the accompaniment of some newspaper criticisms, the House of Representatives was dissolved on 1 November; polling took place on 30 November. When the dust of battle cleared, the Government emerged with a majority of twenty-two.

Unexpectedly, I now arrived at one of the turning points of my life. Although there were further ameliorations of policy I wished to accomplish in Immigrations, after the best part of six years in administering that department one felt like a change. Menzies, in reconstructing the ministry, thought likewise. During the second week of December, he sent for me and in the friendliest possible way, offered me the alternative of continuing in the Cabinet with a different portfolio, or proceeding to Britain as Australian High Commissioner. Sir Eric Harrison had told him he wished to come home; accordingly Menzies proposed I should take up the post in April, 1964. I asked for time to consult my wife and children. Acceptance would involve a big upheaval, especially as the Prime Minister indicated I might well serve longer than the initial five years, provided the Liberal party remained in power. He requested my decision one way or the other in forty-eight hours, as, if I preferred to leave the Cabinet, a successor must be found. I returned immediately to *Arbury* from where, after a family conference, I telephoned my acceptance of London.

A few days later, Menzies asked to see me in Canberra. When I entered his office, his face looked like a thunder-cloud. Harrison, he said, was insisting on completing his extended term until October, despite pleadings from both Menzies and Holt. What was he to do? If I continued in Cabinet for a further six months this would necessitate a replacement he wished to avoid so soon after an election (by that time his own retirement was only two years distant). Appreciating his predicament I said I would stand aside, but would none the less like to sail for England in April or May so that my children could settled in schools by September, the opening of the British academic year. We would spend most of the intervening time on the Continent so as not to embarrass the Harrisons. The Prime Minister leapt out of his chair with excitement, slapped me on the back, and thankfully agreed. And so it was that the announcement of the new administration, on 18 December, proclaimed my forthcoming appointment as High Commissioner, and Townley as Ambassador to Washington. Not long afterwards, Barwick left the ministry of Foreign Affairs to become Chief Justice of the High Court.

The same day – because in politics once decisions are made the consequences usually follow quickly – I handed over my responsibilities to my successor, Hubert Opperman, at a hastily arranged ceremony on the lawn of the Immigration department. The suddenness of it all made me feel sad. After such a long and friendly association with my officers, parting came as a wrench. Since my advent to office early in 1958 we had brought approximately three quarters of a million people to Australia; the migration laws had been reformed and humanised; new recruiting posts in Britain and Europe had been created; some important variations of the hitherto strict Anglo-European policy in favour of worth Asian settlers were introduced; I repeatedly urged new citizens to maintain their European traditions and culture to Australia's enrichment. It had been a long innings, exceeded only by Harold Holt, but despite spirited public controversies on individual cases affecting entry and deportation, the results proved to the nation's advantage.

~ 4 ~

The High Commissionership necessitated relinquishing my seat in Parliament, which I did on 23 April 1964. A few days later the South Australian Government purchased *Arbury Park*, thus concluding a painful, long, drawn-out controversy. Leaving *Arbury* was an emotional experience for us all. I had lived there for nearly thirty years; so much of it was my youthful creating, my first child I have often called it; but the determination of the State Cabinet to construct the principal freeway of the State in front of the house, and across both deer park and water meadows within a few yards of my mother's memorial chapel, destroyed the soul of the property as a peaceful rural retreat.

We sailed from Sydney in the P & O *Canberra* on 2 May, on a voyage which led us to Honolulu, Los Angeles, San Francisco, Acapulco, the Panama Canal, Nassau and finally Southampton on 9 June. In London, our priority lay in arranging schools for the children: Montreux, Switzerland for the two elder girls, Radley for Alexander and a preparatory school in Kensington for Una. The next two months we travelled on the Continent, re-appearing in London in September. An interesting assignment from Canberra came that month when Paul Hasluck, then Foreign Minister, asked me to represent Australia in Malta at their independence ceremonies. We were joined there by Walter Crocker, our Ambassador in The Hague, and with Mary, spent five days in smoothly organised official entertainments provided by Dr Borg Oliver's friendly Government, the admirable Governor-General Sir Maurice Dorman, and underlying all, the welcoming, amiable Maltese people.

By 24 October the day at last dawned for me to assume my duties as Australian High Commissioner. The official residence, then as now, was *Stoke Lodge*, 45 Hyde Park Gate. It is a pleasantly situated house in a quiet cul-de-sac, close to Kensington Gardens. As a private town house it would be delightful; for an embassy of an important country it is inconvenient, and too small. Domestically we had a difficult beginning, entering a house without servants, faced with our first official dinner party for the Australian and British foreign ministers the following week. The next morning that most distinguished and experienced of all Australia's High Commissioners, Lord Bruce, telephoned his good wishes with offers to help. 'Remember,' he said, 'That our British friends, with all their qualities are as cunning as rats.' Rather startled by this warning from such an Anglophile, I came to realise its truth the ensuing eight years.

But there were no personal problems at Australia House. Although I had been disappointed at being compelled to take over in their entirety, Sir Eric Harrison's personal staff, the two senior men could not have been more helpful. Harold MacDonald MBE, the private secretary, had served the two previous High Commissioners: he quickly convinced me he possessed a loyalty, efficiency, expertise and administrative ability which should have earned him a much higher post. The principal secretary-typist, Mrs Watts MBE, was also rich in experience, having worked in the High Commissioner's Office since the days of Lord Bruce. Initially she viewed me with some reserve, but soon we developed an excellent relationship. For the incessant flow of dictation she typed, as well as many of my speeches throughout eight years, she earned my undying gratitude. In the wider administrative hierarchy I was fortunate enough in the advice and wisdom of one of Australia's top civil servants, Sir Allen Brown. Formerly head of the Prime Minister's department and Cabinet Secretary, he had already enjoyed five and a half years as Deputy High Commissioner. He remained another six months before moving to Japan as

Australian Ambassador. The Official Secretary, who is the chief administrative officer, was WR Cumming, MVO, an able if somewhat taciturn man. He too gave me every possible assistance.

Australia House in those days was a compendious establishment directly controlled by the Prime Minister and his department in Canberra. No fewer than twenty-two departments of state were represented, the most significant being Foreign (then called External) Affairs, Immigration, trade and a sizeable military mission alternately headed by senior servicemen from the navy, army and air force. Altogether eleven hundred people worked in the High Commission: this figure included our provincial, Scottish and Ulster offices. Approximately four hundred of these were employed in migration activities. It became impossible to accommodate so many in Australia House; other premises in various parts of London had been rented, arrangements not productive of efficiency. So early in 1965, at the instigation of Sir Allen Brown, we persuaded the Government to take a long lease of nine floors of a new building off *The Strand*, merely a minute's walk away. This I named *Canberra House*, and in it we centralised departments hitherto dispersed.

I soon found the role of High Commissioner fascinating, glamorous, but as arduous as the life of a cabinet minister, except for the constant travelling the latter entails. The Queen received Mary and me at Buckingham Palace on 30 October with the utmost ease and charm. I told her of our intention to buy a country house and asked her about *Windlesham Moor* where she and Prince Philip had partly lived when first married. *Windlesham* had been offered to us recently. She thought we would do better by going further afield, especially as we were looking for a place in real country and with some land. She showed great sympathy over *Arbury*, and seemed amazed in a country the size of Australia at the State Government's insistence on bisecting the estate by their freeway. This was the first of many enthralling occasions at the Palace and at Windsor, and of tremendous kindness and friendship shown to us by the Queen and Prince Philip.

In Britain the Government had changed almost simultaneously with my accession to office. After thirteen years of uninterrupted rule, the Conservatives lost the October general election by five seats. On 15th October, Sir Alec Douglas-Home resigned to give way to Harold Wilson, Labor's victorious leader. The first obligation on every head of mission on assuming his post is to make a series of official calls. This begins with the Marshal of the Diplomatic Corps, then Lord Cairns, at his office in the courtyard of Buckingham Palace. My next call was on the new Prime Minister at 10 Downing Street. A secretary ushered me into the historic Cabinet Room where the Prime Minister was sitting in his customary place at the oblong cabinet table. I handed him a letter of commendation from Menzies; a friendly talk ensued during which Wilson spoke warmly about Menzies, and said that one of his objectives would be to strengthen the Commonwealth. He spoke appreciatively of his months in Western Australia between the age of nine and ten where his uncle, Sir Harold Seddon, was President of the Legislative Counsel, and where he still had a number of relations. I have written at length elsewhere of my contacts and negotiations where British Prime Ministers and Cabinet Ministers during 1964 to 1972, and their dealings with our Australia counterparts. The oncoming years were to prove turbulent, a period of decline for Britain, and despite all my efforts a weakening of Anglo-Australian as well as Commonwealth ties. The reasons for this radical reorientation in Britain's alignments were political and economic, allied to a fading national ambition: no diplomacy could withstand such a tidal wave.

For a new High Commissioner or Ambassador the business of calling on ministers, diplomatic colleagues and Court officers is protracted where as in London, more than one hundred and thirty missions are accredited to the Court of St James. One's other duties preclude calling on all of them; it is arduous in that complex community to achieve more than two each day. My practice was to call first on the doyen of the Diplomatic Corps, next on my fellow Commonwealth High Commissioners, then on Ambassadors from countries such as the United States, those of Western Europe, Japan, Turkey with each of whom Australia had particular interests whether strategic, political, commercial, migratory or cultural. Fortunately the time-honoured custom of Ambassadors returning calls is falling into disuse, but the protocol of making a first call has practical value in that it enables a newcomer to become acquainted with his diplomatic colleagues which would otherwise be difficult in a world centre such as London.

The activities of a High Commissioner of a principal Commonwealth country are multifarious. In a mission the size of Australia House there is always day-to-day administration to attend to. Harmonious relations with the six State Agents-Generals are desirable, though not in every case easy to achieve. I continued my immediate predecessor's practice of periodical conferences, enlisting their co-operation, opening doors of information in whatever of our departments they sought assistance. On the whole, throughout my eight years we formed a happy group, aiming at co-operating in the overall interests of Australia. It was also important to keep in touch with senior officials within *Australia* and *Canberra Houses*. For this purpose we held monthly meetings at which many of us pooled useful information: from 1966 onwards the summer gathering at *Oare House,* preceded by a buffet luncheon, became one of the pleasures of the year. But it is the representational and political (in the broadest sense) side of the work which counts most. Of importance, too, are communications and contacts with the Palace. In April 1965, the Queen invited us to Windsor for a night. We were given a suite of rooms in the King Edward VIII tower, hung with pictures by Canaletto and other masters. The

Queen and Prince Philip welcomed us in one of the drawing rooms in the late afternoon; a dinner party followed attended by Prince Charles, Princess Anne, the Lord Chancellor Lord Gardiner and his wife, Lord and Lady Slim and other interesting personalities. After dinner, the Queen showed a number of us the library, and some of its celebrated manuscripts. When I work up in the morning it was my fifty-fifth birthday.

The year proved eventful and successful except for two sad circumstances, one public and the other personal. Late in January Sir Winston Churchill died. Eight days afterwards in a bitter weather, a magnificently organised State funeral followed in St Paul's, attended by leaders from all over the world. From our seats in the Cathedral we observed the passage of the great: the nonchalant hauteur of General de Gaulle, President Johnson – tall and assured, Harold Wilson – short and undistinguished, Sir Robert Menzies – prepared to deliver his moving panegyric. Universal mourning encompassed the realm.

My mother-in-law, Lady Gosse, had visited us for most of the winter. In May, a few weeks after her return to Adelaide, she suddenly died. A little later I took Mary and Una for four days respite (covering the spring holiday weekend) to one of our favourite resorts, the Trianon Palace Hotel overlooking the park at Versailles. No sooner had we arrived than a telephone rang from London. My heart sank, fearing some crisis demanding my return forthwith. Instead, Frank Boyle – one of my senior offices – told me the Commonwealth Office wished to know whether I would accept a knighthood of the Order of the British Empire. Elated by this news we drank a bottle of champagne; the announcement appeared in the Queen's Birthday list on 12 June.

Five days later a Commonwealth Prime Ministers' Conference opened in the sparkling chandelier room of Marlborough House. This was the first of four I have attended as one of Australia's delegates. Sir Robert Menzies and Paul Hasluck were the principal Australian representatives; Harold

Wilson mostly chaired the assembly. These gatherings I have discussed in my book on Prime Ministers; they were some of the most interesting, and at times disturbing, experiences of my career. Becoming acquainted with Commonwealth leaders was enlightening: Lester Pearson from Canada, smooth and assured; the ascetic Shastri from India; East African presidents Kaunda, Nyerere and Prime Minister (later President) Obote – these three personally courteous but exuding vitriol at the conference table: Malawi's wizened, eloquent, realistic ruler Dr Hastings Banda; the ill-fated Sir Abubakar Tafawa Belewa of Nigeria; Archbishop Makarios from Cyprus – always moving silently, sedately, seldom speaking in his black head dress, mysterious, unfathomable; New Zealand's sonorous Sir Keith Holyoake whose utterances, despite their amiability, reminded me of the psalmist's 'sounding brass and tinkling cymbal'; President Ayub Khan of Pakistan and his foreign Minister ZA Bhutto, destined to die on the gallows in 1979. However deplorable his end, Bhutto in those days, aged only thirty-seven, looked and sounded aggressive, combining hostile criticisms of Britain with unfriendliness towards nations such as my own.

This conference is memorable for two decisions: the establishment of the Commonwealth Secretariat, and a body designed to promote professional links called the Commonwealth Foundation on which I represented Australia until 1972. Inevitably, I had much to do with the Secretariat from then onwards and its inaugural Secretary-Genera, the Canadian Arnold Smith.

Not long afterwards a significant change occurred in British politics. Sir Alec Douglas-Home resigned as leader of the Conservatives. In June he took me to lunch at the Carlton Club, and in private conversation doubted whether he would continue. I begged him not to throw his hand in (subsequently his wife told me she was of the same opinion) but dissident back-bench pressure persuaded him the party would best be served by finding a substitute. Two were waiting in the wings, Reginald Maudling and Edward Heath. The ballot favoured Heath.

Before the year was out the Rhodesian problem erupted with Prime Minister Ian Smith's unilateral declarations of independence in November. Thus began the most prolonged and contentious of all Commonwealth issues.

For our family – and to the advantage of Australian representation in Britain – in the autumn we found the sort of country house we had been seeking. This is the *Oare Estate* in north Wiltshire. A late Queen Anne manor-house in design (though built in 1740, with later additions this century) it stands on the edge of the Vale of Pewsey, overlooking nearly one hundred acres of park and woods, with extensive garden surrounding the house and sweeping views of the Marlborough Downs. I have long believed in the value of country house diplomacy, where delicate matters can be freely discussed without formality, and without secretaries taking notes. Not only did *Oare House* become a home for our children to grow up in, but a place where we could entertain on weekends, much more suitably than at Stoke Lodge. I bought *Oare* at a private auction in London in October; we moved in the following February. During the ten years we live there, thousands of Australians visited us, including four of our Prime Ministers, a stream of ministers and parliamentary colleagues from Canberra, Labor leaders such as Gough Whitlam, Clyde Cameron, Lance Barnard, to say nothing of British ministers, members of the Royal family and English friends from near and far. With a heavy heart financial circumstances compelled us to relinquish *Oare* in January 1976, but it played an invaluable part in our official and private lives.

Throughout 1965 we fulfilled public engagements not merely in London, but in Scotland, Ulster (where my old friend Lord Brookeborough still reigned as Prime Minister) and English provincial cities. One of the temptations a diplomat must overcome is becoming too involved with the London scene. In these vast cross-roads of the world so much occurs demanding one's presence. Yet to succumb is to neglect an important part of representational duties. Looking back on my time, I feel I should have moved about the United Kingdom more, particularly in Scotland and Wales. The reception accorded a visiting High Commissioner in those parts is very rewarding. However, one of the highlights that year was Mary's launching of HMAS *Oxley* on 24 September at Greenock on the Clyde. Sir Robert Menzies asked her to do this. *Oxley* is the first of the Oberon class submarines built by Scots for the Royal Australian Navy. The launching, on a cold morning, proceeded without blemish; several hundred guests were then regaled with a splendid lunch in the Town Hall. The chairman of the company presented Mary with four silver birds, which she gracefully acknowledged in a well-delivered speech. In later years we attended three more of these ceremonies, performed by Princess Marina, Princess Alexandra and Lady Slim.

In London I received a pleasant compliment beginning towards the end of 1964 and completed in 1965. The Tallow chandlers, one of the ancient City companies, admitted me to their livery as a fully-fledged member. This involved my being given the Freedom of the City of London, a distinction I cherish. In September the Butchers Company made me an honorary freeman. I now belong to three of these historic societies, the Woolmen having created me an honorary freeman in 1974.

January 1966 marked the opening of a fresh chapter in Australian political history. Sir Robert Menzies, aged seventy-one, retired after sixteen continuous years as Prime Minister. My good friend Harold Holt succeeded him. From my angle in London, none of the five Australian Prime Ministers during my High Commissionership was so friendly, so appreciative, so encouraging as Holt. For me, personally, this was not such an eventful year as the one before, but it began a period of intense diplomatic activity in British-Australian relations centring around defence, the Common market, and immigration restrictions as I have recounted elsewhere. In March, Harold Wilson seized a favourable opportunity of improving his tenuous parliamentary situation; the result gave him an election majority of close to one hundred. And not long before he advised the Queen to appoint Menzies as Lord Warden of the Cinque Ports, vacant since the death of Churchill. In steaming heat, on 20 July, the great man, more impressive than ever in his Lord Warden's uniform, was installed in a series of ceremonies at Dover. In contrast with a singularly tactless sermon from Dr Ramsay, Archbishop of Canterbury, at the church service, Menzies later in the day made one of the most moving speeches of his career. His appointment aroused high satisfaction in England.

By the summer, Wilson executed on of his somersaults: Britain would now seek membership of the EEC. We were also worried whether he would keep his promise to me and to others of maintaining British defence commitments east of Suez. Throughout the year I used appropriate occasions in public speeches to urge the Government to retain their historic Commonwealth connections, which of course they would jettison by moving helter-skelter into Europe whilst simultaneously withdrawing from the Persian Gulf and South-East Asia. Not only did I believe such a course would damage British interests both politically and commercially; I was anxious to stake a claim for special consideration for Australia, and indeed all the Old Commonwealth. This latter point a section of the Sydney and Melbourne press never seemed to understand.

Early September saw the assembly in London for another Commonwealth Prime Minister's conference. It met at Marlborough House between 6 September and 15 September, and was the stormiest and the worst of the four I have attended. Rhodesia provided the fiercest area of contention, with all the Africans, except the realistic Banda of Malawi, urging Britain to use force against Ian Smith. As in 1965, Harold Wilson, the chairman, showed immense skill, patience and phlegmatic in face of African and Caribbean provocation, which most men would have found intolerable. For Holt, this was his first and – as a tragedy decreed – his only appearance in his role of Prime Minister at these gatherings. Occasionally he deputised for Wilson in the chair, displaying his usual conciliation and tact. The Africans quickly came to like him, as did the other delegations. Hasluck, still our Foreign Minister, myself and Bunting (in that order) made up the balance of our team. Compared with the year before some new faces appeared. Shastri, from India, in the meantime had died; Sir Abubakar Tafawn Balewa from Nigeria, had been murdered. Their substitutes were Swaran Singh and my London diplomatic colleague Brigadier Ogundipe. We were spared the argumentative Kaunda from Zambia; his representative, Simon Kapwepwe, proved even more abusive. Kapwepwe bristled with fanaticism, and an unconcealed dislike of Britain. Years later, in 1978, he challenged Kaunda for the Zambian presidency. Kaunda replied by proscribing all other candidates for the position.

As the year drew to a close I applied to go home on leave. In a quickly changing world it is most necessary for diplomats to return regularly to their country. The custom was for the High Commissioner to be granted leave after two and a half years; this contrasted with annual visits home by my American and Canadian colleagues. For geographical reasons the European ambassadors were even better placed. Nowadays, I would urge more frequent visitations by my successors. There is no substitute for on-the-spot investigation and personal contacts within one's own country. We left London on 18 January 1967, taking Stella and Una with us, travelling from Naples to Fremantle in the *Canberra*. The Suez Canal was still open, and being a fast ship the voyage took only sixteen days. I know of no pleasanter journey in the world than a sea-trip between the Mediterranean and Western Australia. It provided a refreshing preparation for the tour I had planned. Throughout most of February and

March we visited every State so that I could talk with State Premiers and Ministers; there were useful opportunities for public speeches and press interviews – on this occasion the press reflected a most friendly light. In addition, there was work to be done in Canberra where the Prime Minister's department gave me an office, secretary and much assistance.

Towards the end of March we flew from Sydney to Vancouver and crossed Canada – still snowbound – in the disappointing Canadian Pacific railway, as far as Ottawa. Thanks to the kindness of our High Commissioner, Sir Kenneth Bailey, we spent a useful two days in this attractive city, and then took the night train to New York. Here too we became greatly indebted to our energetic and popular Consul-General Sir Reginald Sholl, AC. Through him we met the mayor, John Lindsay, a man of unusual personal charm, and his equally appealing wife. They entertained us at the official house, *Gracie Mansion*, built in the American colonial style, whilst another evening Lindsay and I made speeches at the splendid dinner given by the Sholls. In New York we were joined by Alexander and Angela, then on school holidays. Together we crossed the Atlantic in the *Queen Elizabeth* where we found aboard our good friends Anthony and Clarissa Avon. On 7 April we docked at Southampton and so back to duty in London.

Less than a fortnight later, Konrad Adenauer, Germany's most celebrated post-war Chancellor, died. Holt asked me to represent Australia at his funeral in the Rhineland. Our Ambassador in Bonn, FJ Blakeney, invited me to stay at the embassy in Bad Godesberg on the banks of the Rhine, which surely must be the best situated of all Australia's diplomatic houses in the world. Apart from mourning the old leader, the occasion provided a meeting of world figures. President Johnson flew from America; de Gaulle came to pay tribute to a statesman whom he regarded as a friend of France; Wilson represented Britain. The obsequies began in the Bundestag at Bonn. Then the cortege moved to Cologne, where a requiem was sung in what to me is always a cathedral of uplifting inspirations. From here, the coffin was placed on a barge on the Rhine, and so began a stately procession upstream to Rheindorf for burial. From the embassy garden the Ambassador and I witnessed this unforgettable scene - the arrangements were curiously imperfect. The Adenauer family, in the Bundestag especially, were not accorded places and priorities which in English speaking countries would be regarded as their due. When departing they were jostled by the crowd. Traffic arrangements seemed badly planned. The ceremonies, designed I was told to rival those of Churchill in 1965, did not flow smoothly. That evening the German Government gave a buffet dinner, with exquisite local wines, and in this international gathering many useful contacts occurred. These entertainments continued the next day with customary German hospitality.

On May Day it fell to me to open Australia's Migration Office at Bristol designed to serve the West Country and Wales. The occasion seemed opportune to plead for retention of British bases East of Suez, and generally to place primary emphasis on ties with the Old Commonwealth and the United States rather than with Europe. The speech was well reported in the London and provincial press, but not so sensationally as the three subsequent speeches I made in the autumn: one in London at a P & O reception in the *Mansion House*, the second at a Royal Commonwealth society luncheon in Bath given every 11 October to honour the birthday of Admiral Philip, the third at Liverpool on 23 October. My efforts to alert British public opinion as to the consequences of projected British actions were reinforces by Sir Robert Menzies' powerful address delivered at Ditchley on 28 July. Alas! History was to show that nothing could deflect the Labor Government and a large section of the Conservative party from their chosen course.

During the year, two notable Australian figures died: first Lord Baillieu, then Lord Bruce. I was asked to read the lesson at each of their memorial services. However, they were old men. Not so our Prime Minister. Early in the morning of 16 December, my Deputy John Knott (now Sir John) telephoned me at *Oare* to say that Harold Holt was missing in the sea on the Bass Strait side of Portsea. This proved a tragedy for the whole of Australia as well as for his family and friends. It was a sad loss to me personally: sixty is too young for an apparently healthy man to die. The Prince of Wales, Harold Wilson and Edward Heath left Heathrow in a special aircraft on 20 December for Melbourne to attend a memorial service in StPaul's Cathedral on 22; having farewelled them on their departure, protocol demanded that I should welcome their return on the 23 December. In the New Year we at Australia house organised a memorial service in London. I chose Westminster Abbey to emphasise his political career and his distinguished role in the Commonwealth Parliamentary Association. Zara Holt behaved stoically; Bill Baddeley, recently Dean of Brisbane, gave the address; the lesson was read by me. I have never seen the Abbey more crowded, and the organisation showed a much smoother efficiency than on a similar occasion for Sir Robert Menzies in 1978.

John McEwen, as deputy Prime Minister, immediately and rightly stepped in to Harold Holt's shoes: but not for long. Being leader of the smaller branch of the coalition, the Liberals insisted on finding their own man. In this they ignored the national interest, because McEwen was by far the ablest and most experienced minister in both parties. Their choice surprised me, and I think many people. John Gorton, a senator, gained the succession. He quickly resigned from the Senate to enter the House of Representatives for Holt's seat of Higgins. And so began a turbulent and unconventional chapter of political history.

The new Prime Minister introduced not only his own idiosyncratic style of government, but Sir Lenox Hewitt as head of his department in place of the popular, respected, experienced Sir John Bunting. Hewitt years before had served in Australia

House as Official Secretary with a high reputation for efficiency. At this time I hardly knew him, but we quickly established a rapport and despite his reputation of being difficult to get on with, we enjoyed for the most part a harmonious relationship.

On the personal level, one of the most interesting events of 1968 took place in Hamburg. There, on the 5 June, Mary launched the first of the express container ships for the Australian trade. She named her *Encounter Bay*, a seascape with family connections for both of us.

Built for the OCL line, a consortium partly owned by P & O, the ceremony and subsequent luncheon banquet at the Atlantic Hotel were marred by rain, the German builders omitting to provide any cover for this contingency. A defect in the slipway was rectified only in minutes to spare before the ebbing tide on the Elbe would have prevented the 29,000 ton ship sliding into the water. Much as I admire many contemporary Germans, they seem to contain a curious streak of inefficiency where one least expects to find it. The incident reminded me of blunders in Dr Adenauer's funeral arrangements fourteen months before.

During the middle of the year we made some useful visits in the provinces. In July I opened a new factory for Rocla Pipes at St Helens, Lancashire, which provided an opportunity to plead for continued British investment in Australia. Shortly afterward I performed the same office for the new Australian Centre in Leeds where we were warmly greeted by the Lord Mayor and prominent citizens. We stayed subsequently in Manchester, spending a fascinating morning inspecting the port and part of the famous ship canal. The following month found us in Glasgow again (by then we were coming to know it quite well) for Princess Alexandra's launching of the fourth Oberon class submarine. Early November we flew to Northern Ireland on a four day official visit. Terrence O'Neill (now Lord O'Neill of the Maine) had succeeded Lord Brookeborough as Prime Minister; I had known him more than thirty years before when briefly in Adelaide as an ADC to Sir Malcolm Barclay-Harvey, the Governor, and with cordial hospitality he entered us at a Government luncheon at Stormont. An easy, affable man, our exchanges of views were uninhibited and most pleasant. In Belfast I made a carefully considered speech on Australia-Ulster relations to the Royal Overseas League which achieved good reportage in the loca newspapers. After inspecting our Belfast Migration Office we spent a short weekend at Colebrook with the Brookeboroughs. Sadly, this was the last occasion we saw Cynthia at home; she died in March 1970, and with her went so much of the essence of Colebrooke.

The year 1969 opened in London in a flurry of activity, preparing for another Commonwealth Prime Ministers Conference at Marlborough House on 7 January.

Once again, battles raged over Rhodesia, with the Africans, except Banda, and their Caribbean allies, still attacking Britain for not using force. Two new major personalities graced the Conference table: Pierre Trudeau, Canadian Prime Minister since 1968, and Indira Gandhi, already Prime Minister of India for three years. Trudeau deliberately played his role in a low key. With disarming candour he declared he did not know much about the Commonwealth – he had come to listen and to learn. Mrs Gandhi's attitude seemed listless. She remained for merely three out of eight sitting days, appearing uninterested in the proceedings, giving the impression that the Commonwealth mattered little in her scheme of things. Both were charming people socially: Mrs Gandhi's good looks and manners gave no hint of dictatorial practices to come. And it was easy to appreciate Trudeau's electoral appeal with his boyish frankness and winsome manners. At Singapore in 1971 he was much more active and outspoken.

John Gorton and his wife, accompanied by the agile Lenox Hewitt arrived only the morning before this contentious conclave began. Having sat first with Menzies in 1965, then with Holt at the 1966 Conference, one awaited Gorton's performance with some trepidation. These apprehensions were quickly dispelled: he and Wilson soon became friends; the argumentative Africans liked him; his utterances and conduct during the discussions were impeccable. The British, still peerless as hosts, staged their customary series of splendid entertainments. After the conference we gave one of our most useful diplomatic dinners for the Gortons and the Wilsons, their respective private secretary Sir Michael Adeane, a leading industrialist and the Principal of Brasenose, together with their wives. A few nights later, at an Australian Club banquet at the Dorchester, Gorton received a standing ovation as his speech concluded.

It was during this visit that Gorton agreed to an extension of my term as High Commissioner for a further year as from the 25 October. But he did not announce my reappointment until 24 November.

On several occasions this year I tried to incorporate in speeches encouragement for, and appreciation of, Britain. Public morale was sagging; words of praise from a friend might be helpful. The London press reacted most favourably – such action seemed a useful emollient to the criticisms in Australia's interest I had made over British defence withdrawals, the Government's new-found love for the Common Market, and their immigration restrictions. But at home certain journalists attacked me for being pro-British, and for not speaking out enough for Australia. This merely confirmed my earlier experiences of the lack of understanding of some newspaper commentators who seldom take the trouble to interview their victim and discover the thinking of those they so roundly criticise.

The glamorous event of 1969 was Prince Charles' investiture by the Queen as Prince of Wales at Carnarvon Castle. We travelled in a special train packed with guests from al over the world. Although 2 July, the day was cool and showery, but the weather did not detract from artistic pageantry and faultless organisation. The scene in the Castle courtyard was unforgettable. Neither bomb scares nor (as we learnt afterwards) the Queen's temperature of 101 degrees marred the ceremony. Yet to me the occasion seemed tinged with artificiality; it lacked the meaningfulness of a coronation and some other royal activities.

Early in the autumn I applied for home leave. The Canberra scene had changed much since the early months of 1967, and talks with the Gorton Cabinet and senior public servants seemed necessary. With the Prime Minister's concurrence we sailed with Stella in the *Oriana* on 4 November, this time via South Africa, the Suez Canal being closed since the Israeli-Egyptian war. My colleague, the South African Ambassador, Dr Hendrik Luttig, arranged for us to be looked after in Capetown and Durban. In both cities we were treated to an imaginative programme, particularly in the Cape where we were taken to the Paarl district, Stellenbosch, and the Simonstown naval base. At a press interview in Durban I expressed friendship for South Africa (openly disagreeing with apartheid), and predicted good Australian-South African relations. Events since then, the hostility of the Whitlam administration, unwisely continued by Malcolm Fraser, have falsified those hopes; however, my impressions, albeit fleeting and perhaps superficial, were ones of strength in the South African economy. I said then, and I still believe, this controversial country is the strongest part of the African continent with whom it is Australia's and Britain's interest to be friends.

Arriving in Perth on 25 November we stayed three days with Sir Douglas and Lady Kendrew at Government House. Useful talks followed with the Premier, Sir David Brand and his dynamic lieutenant Charles Court. As on my previous leaver, we visited all States as well as Canberra. In South Australia my friend Henry Rymill lent us our old family summer house, *Glenalta*, for Christmas. Ten days before, we were joined by our other children in Canberra on school holidays, with Angela now engaged to Charles Clauson. The Governor of Victoria and Lady Delacombe generously invited all of us to stay with them in Melbourne; Sir Henry Bolte, the Premier, gave us a reception. In Hobart on 2 January, Sir Edric and Lady Bastyan showed us similar hospitality in perhaps Austrlian's most attractive Government House. These four days in Hobart coincided with Edward Heath's winning the Sydney-Hobart Yacht Race, and during one night at Government House we all conversed intimately with him over a wide range of subjects. My periods in Canberra were timely. John Gorton, fresh from his victory as Prime Minister in the November elections (though with a much reduced majority) seemed firmly entrenched for three years, McMahon had become Foreign Minister, Fraser Minister for Defence. One could sense no hint of the discords to come.

Our journey back to England was extraordinarily interesting. From Sydney we flew to Hong Kong for three days, then on to Tokyo for the best part of a week in Japan. Sir Allen Brown, the Australian Ambassador and Lady Brown, could not have been more helpful. He invited us to stay in his embassy house, provided us with a car to visit Lake Hakone and other places, and detailed a most informative second secretary to accompany us to Kyoto and Osaka where we inspected the Australian exhibit at the World Fair. I had not seen Japan since my three months there as a boy of ten, nor until now had I wanted to go there as a result of military misadventures between 1941 and 1945. Trying to understand Japan at the beginning of the 1970s, meeting a number of Japanese, looking at the vast agglomeration of the younger generation, all combined to dissolve much of the war poison remaining in my mind. Henceforth, this became a country to which I am always glad to return.

The last country we visited briefly was India. In New Delhi, where we stayed two days, our High Commission arranged for us to be shown over the Parliament, parts of old Delhi, as well as historic monuments. On another day we drove to Agra, staying the night in this alluring city. This enabled us to see the Taj Mahal by moonlight (the moon was nearly full) as well as in the morning and the late afternoon. I like the morning light best, but contemplating this exquisite work of art at any time evokes within me profound emotion. The Taj, if nothing else, will ever magnetise me back to India.

We returned to London on 15 February. On 26 February we had the honour of entertaining the Queen, Prince Charles, and Princess Anne to diner at Stoke Lodge. The Queen was shortly afterwards leaving for Australia; it is her custom to dine with a High Commissioner before travelling to his country. Gracious and sparkling, she delighted our three elder children by her ease of manner as well as the few friends there to meet her.

Our next big occasion was a family one. On 3 April, Angela married Charles Clauson, then a lieutenant in the Welsh Guards, in the Henry VII chapel of Westminster Abbey. The service was simple, moving, enhanced not only by the singing of the Abbey choir amidst such architectural beauty, but by Eric Abbott, Dean of Westminster, who married them. His homily should have been recorded for future generations. Afterwards, we received two hundred guests at *Stoke Lodge* where a marquee in the garden provided space beyond the capacity of the house. The bride and bridegroom were young: Angela only twenty, Charles twenty-three, but theirs is the model of a happy union.

April also saw the inauguration in England of a series of events celebrating the bicentenary of Captain Cook's discovery of eastern Australia. These spread out over the next two months. For me, the focal point lay at Whitby, where Cook grew up. On 20 April I unveiled a plaque given by the Australian Government attached to Cook's memorial cairn overlooking the North Sea, and later attended a large official luncheon given by the Mayor. Through the kindness of the Lord Lieutenant, the Marquis of Normandy, we stayed at Mulgrave Castle, his family seat, nearby. Unquestionably one of England's great houses it is also one of the best maintained. Fortunately he and his charming wife, one of the notable Guinness sisters, possess the means to live in the manner of people of their rank in the earliest part of this century. His gallery of Greek and Roman sculptures is possibly the finest private collection in the land; the Mulgrave Library, too, is magnificent.

In May I visited Brussels for two days to address an international investment conference. Brussels is my least favourite European capital city, but in 1970 its atmosphere had not become so impersonally internationalised as today. Irresistibly, my speech dealt with the EEC and its likely effects on Australia after Britain joined. These financiers, drawn from most western European countries, listened politely, asked questions, were friendly – but were unconvinced. Australia, they felt, seemed a rich nation: it could look after itself without undue disturbance to her economy.

The spotlight next played on British politics. More than four years had elapsed since the previous general election. With only another ten months to run, Wilson, sensing further personal electoral victory in the air, advised the Queen to dissolve the House of Commons. Voting was fixed for 18 June – Waterloo Day – not, I thought, a propitious omen for a Labor leader. The opinion polls all (except one) indicated socialist success. Many of my Conservative friends were despondent. Talking to the Prime Minister at the *Trooping the Colour* on 13 June, the question in his mind was not who would win but the size of the Government's majority. By eleven o'clock on the night of 18 June the message was clear: Wilson had miscalculated; Health had secured a substantial majority. The following afternoon removal vans stood outside 10 Downing Street, loading the vanquished Prime Minister's belongings.

Not long afterwards John Gorton asked me whether I would accept a second extension of my term in London, until late October 1971. To this I agreed.

The death of a great man cast a shadow over Christmas. Field Marshal Viscount Slim was not only Australia's most distinguished, most successful, most admired Governor-General, but Lord Mountbatten considered him the ablest general of World War II. His family paid me the high compliment of being one of the ten pall-bearers at his funeral in St George's Chapel, Windsor, on 22 December. On a mild, grey morning we marched through the streets of this ancient town behind the gun-carriage bearing his coffin, and so to the chapel where Robin Woods, Dean of Windsor, conducted the service. The Field Marshal would have approved of the perfection of the arrangements which were carried out with a precision and dignity expressive of England at her best.

Another memorable event now occurred involving an international journey. In mid-January 1971, the Commonwealth Prime Ministers assembled at Singapore for a conference presaged with difficulties. I wanted particularly to attend this gathering, the first since the change of government in Britain seven months earlier. By that time I had come to know Edward Heath quite well, and to like him. Sir Alec Douglas-Home, the Foreign and Commonwealth Secretary, was a friend; my relations with Sir Denis Greenhilll, the permanent head of the Foreign and Commonwealth Office, were also cordial. Believing that my lengthening experience in Britain could be useful, I asked Gorton whether he would allow me to join our own delegation. He agreed; Mary could come too. So we set off early in January, calling at Istanbul on the way for two days, and reaching Singapore two days before the conference opened. Nick Parkinson, the Australian High Commissioner in Singapore, invited us to stay with him and his talented wife, and with them we remained for a fortnight. This is not the place to describe what followed: I have dealt at length with this forthright meeting in writing abut Heath and Gorton. Contention raged over Britain's intention to sell some limited military equipment to South Africa, and to a lesser extent Rhodesia. Both of these Prime Ministers distinguished themselves in the debates, as well as on formal occasions outside the conference hall; both having been unfairly attacked by journalists for the part they played. Apparently, in the eyes of a section of the press, it is a crime to defend the interest of one's country.

We broke our flight back to London by a brief call at New Delhi, arriving in time for the annual Australia Day observances. In February, our ever-active Trade department presented a revealing Australian trade fair which generated useful publicity at the opening of which I pointed out the deleterious effect in Anglo-Australian trade when Britain joined the EEC. During the same month the Heath Government promulgated their new restrictive immigration legislation which, if unamended, would be detrimental to Australians and indeed all Commonwealth citizens, irrespective of whether they were the Queen's subjects or not. I resumed serious negotiations with Reginald Maudling, the Home Secretary, on this issue which I had initiated some months before. My protestations were helped by his friendly feelings – this often criticised man, once Heath's rival for the Tory leadership, radiated a sunny personality, and the fact that at this time he had an Australian daughter-in-law. In the result his Government devised the patrial clause, which at least went some way towards softening our resentment. Nevertheless, the Heath Cabinet, by their concentration on the EEC, made the majority of Commonwealth citizens aliens, a sorry commentary on modern Conservative thinking.

Within Australia, political events now took, at least for me, and unexpected turn. In March Gorton lost the support of half the parliamentary Liberal party. Instantly he resigned, and made way for a man he had long disliked. His Foreign Minister, William McMahon. Again, to my surprise, he consented to serve in McMahon's Government as Minister for Defence – five months later McMahon dismissed him. Important administrative changes ensued. McMahon immediately restored Sir John Bunting as Secretary of the Prime Minister's Department, the wisest act of his short-lived period at *The Lodge*. I felt deeply for Gorton who by then, whatever his mistakes in domestic policy, had emerged as a Prime Minister of considerable attainment internationally. As for the Liberals, their desertion of Gorton paved the way for Whitlam's triumph in December 1972.

Gorton came to London again in his demoted role as Defence Minister for the Five Power Defence meeting on 15 and 16 April. The Conservatives, intent on rebuilding a very modest British presence in South-East Asia, in place of Wilson's East of Suez scuttle, convoked this conference under the chairmanship of Lord Carrington, Secretary of State for Defence. The parties involved were, Britain, Australia, New Zealand, Malaysia and Singapore. Despite some difficulties occasioned by Singapore's demand that Australia and New Zealand should pay rent for their service premises, agreement was concluded on Britain, Australia and New Zealand continuing to station forces there after the end of 1971. Furthermore, the latter here pledged themselves to joint consultation with Malaysia and Singapore to decide what measures should be taken if either of them suffered external attack of were threatened by attack. Unfortunately, much of this valuable alliance between five Commonwealth countries was visited by the Whitlam Government's destructive decision in 1973 to withdraw Australian forces from Singapore.

Eleven days later, the South-East Asia Treaty Organisation met in London. This was the second SEATO conference held in London during my term. Nations represented were the United States, Britain, Australia, New Zealand, the Philippines and Thailand with observers from Vietnam. Leslie Bury, our Foreign Minister, led the Australian delegation. I do not recollect any important decisions flowing from Lancaster House where we deliberated. Already most members were privately doubting SEATO's efficacy. But the delegates enjoyed great and artistic entertainment: the conference opening in Inigo Jones' Banqueting Hall, Whitehall; the Foreign Secretary's dinner at Hampton Court Palace; the Queen's banquet at Windsor Castle (where I sat next to Princess Margaret); a buffet support at Guildhall given by the Lord Mayor of London; the Prime Minister's reception at 10 Downing Street. No partners in the modern world could be accorded more majestic hospitality.

For Mary and me, 1971 became a year of glittering occasions. The Queen invited us to her private party at the Palace for Prince Philip's fiftieth birthday on 10 June. It took the form of a dance, which lasted until the early hours of morning. Prince Philip's relations from all over Europe came to London for the purpose; the other guests were his and the Queen's friends. Much more formal was the state visit of the Emperor and Empress of Japan at the beginning of October. Hirohito behaved like an automaton: stiff, unsmiling, emotionless. The Queen gave one of her brilliant banquets at the Palace, at which the old Empress atoned for her consort by being warm and gracious. Next day, when in accord with custom, the Emperor received the High Commissioners and Ambassadors in St James' Palace, he gave me a glare on presentation which was quite startling. His behaviour that night at the Lord Mayor's Guildhall dinner, upon being given the freedom of the City, seemed equally wooden, as if he were one of Madame Tussaud's wax-works animated by some hidden mechanism. From the point of view of the British public, this visit did not succeed; afterwards the Queen told me she found him most difficult to talk to despite the services of a fluent interpreter. Two months later, the King of Afghanistan, also on a state visit, created a happier impression. The usual ceremonies ensued to which we were bidden: a banquet by the Queen, a levee at St James' Palace, a dinner at guildhall. Whilst waiting for the King to arrive, Edward Heath, the Prime Minister, confidentially informed me of a request by the leading Australian personage which astounded me but which he felt I ought to know.

Meanwhile, at the end of September the Australian Government asked me to continue for a further year until 24 October 1972. This constituted my third extension. In accepting, I insisted on its being my last, and to this McMahon agreed. Throughout the summer, both British and Australian newspapers commented frequently and often sensationally on Anglo-Australian relations as affected by Britain joining the

European Community and our worsening position caused by the Heath Government's restrictive immigration laws. To this my speech at Marlborough House on 24 June, at the opening of the conference of the Commonwealth Press Union, contributed. In retrospect I would not withdraw one word of what I said; indeed, all my predictions have come to pass. It was an unhappy, an argumentative, period but in my judgment, plain speaking was vital to protect Australian interest. Otherwise, our claims for special consideration would have gone by default.

Into this uneasy, contentious, but none the less friendly atmosphere entered William McMahon, on his first visit as Prime Minister, between 7 and 13 November. The British, on their part, rolled out the red carpet (as they told me) in an effort to soften hard feelings. McMahon brought with him a diverse entourage: his glamorous wife, Sonia, whom he clearly regarded as his best publicity asset; Dr Coombs, the former Governor of the Commonwealth Reserve Bank, a man of small physical stature but exhibiting a mind of unusual agility an penetration, in political sympathies much more akin to the Labor party than the Liberals; Sir Keith Waller, Secretary of the Department of Foreign Affairs, an able administrator with a manner and voice reminiscent of a British army officer of the 1930s. I was present at most of the formal conferences with British ministers, the most memorable of which was at 10 Downing Street where McMahon, without any previous consultation with me, unfolded propositions to Heath with which I completely disagreed. For instance, to the amazement of Bunting and myself, he announced the transfer of Australia's representation in Britain from that of the Prime Minister's department to Foreign Affairs, a matter not remotely within the jurisdiction of the British Government. Another was his proposal that the distinction between High Commissioners and Ambassadors should be abolished, all heads of missions henceforth to be called Ambassadors. Heath very properly replied that this was a matter for the Queen to decide, that High Commissioners enjoyed preferment and special privileges in Britain and that the whole Commonwealth would need to be consulted.

McMahon proved more successful in his talks at the Foreign Office with Alec Douglas-Home, Denis Greenhill and others, and particularly at the Ministry of Defence, where he expounded Australia's policy with admirable firmness, tact and precision. But his speech at the Prime Minister's artistically arranged official dinner at Downing Street in the midst of a distinguished audience, showed little sensitivity to the occasion. He did better, however, two days later at a luncheon in his honour given by Rupert Murdoch at the Ritz when, in the presence of London's leading newspaper chiefs, Murdoch cruelly declared that his principal guest's soubriquet in Canberra was 'Billy the leak' – a reference to a long-held rumour that he revealed Cabinet deliberations to journalists. McMahon, in replying, ignored this insult, concentrating entirely on his own Government's attitudes, and in this he displayed great dignity in face of provocation. Throughout his five working days in London – I could neither persuade him to stay longer in England nor speak in populous provincial centres such as Manchester or Birmingham – McMahon expressed his desire for British-Australian accord despite current difficulties, supported the Conservatives' mild defence re-entry to South East Asia, asked for consideration of Australia's interest in their negotiations with the EEC. This was a useful visit: him besetting fault, not only in London but throughout his term as Prime Minister, despite unflagging industry, lay in seeking advice from so many quarters that his judgment became confused and sometimes unwise.

My final year, 1972, opened with another leave home, thanks to McMahon's permission. As in the case of Gorton, so now with McMahon as Prime Minister, I wanted to make some assessment of the altered Australian political scene. Being a short visit, and by now few ships, we travelled by air taking Stella with us: first to Kuala Lumpur for two days during which Rowland, our High Commissioner to Malaysia and Sir John Johnston, his British counterpart, were most helpful. We proceeded south to Singapore in a train of unforgettable awfulness, an exercise designed to show Mary some of the terrain we fought over in 1942, but on arrival the kind Parkinsons refreshed us with a night at the High Commission. In Australia, we gravitated between Sydney, Canberra, Melbourne and Adelaide between 12 January and 25 February, concentrating chiefly on Canberra. The press were friendly, but I reiterated a determination to finish my assignment in October. My theme was that people in top positions should not occupy them for too long, that eight years as High Commissioner was long enough. However good a person might be at a job, change was necessary, and this applied with equal force in politics and diplomacy. I am still of that opinion.

Talks with ministers and departmental heads proved fruitful; Bunting and his officers gave me every possible assistance; but in all these weeks the Prime Minister allotted me only half an hour of his time, and then concentrated his conversation on newspaper criticisms of his administration and local affairs. We flew back to London with a short break at Delhi, followed by a brief interlude in Rome where that controversial diplomat Malcolm Booker, then our Ambassador to Italy, showed us warm hospitality. At the end of the first week of March I was back in the saddle at Australia House.

Compared with the seven previous years, my remaining seven months in office were uneventful. More friction occurred over the treatment of Australians coming to Britain. I asked the new Home Secretary, Robert Carr, to direct immigration officials to display more consideration at ports of entry. He is a man of delightful manners, exceptional capacity, revealing at that time promise of ascending higher up the political ladder. I made similar approaches to the Foreign and Commonwealth Secretary, Alec Home. Some improvement resulted – but continuing to treat the Queen's overseas subjects as aliens is corrosive of Commonwealth sentiment and destructive of lingering notions that Britain is the mother country.

In telegrams to McMahon during August I tried to persuade him to accept a quota of Asians, mainly merchants, whom President Amin was expelling from Uganda. This seemed to me a joint Commonwealth responsibility which, in company with the British, Canadians and one or two others, we should share. They would not merely make useful settlers; Australian participation on humanitarian grounds would reap Commonwealth and international advantages. My efforts were fruitless, the Government remained obdurate.

My last official speeches in the provinces were at Portsmouth in September, where the Lord Mayor made a presentation to commemorate the sailing of Governor Phillip's First Fleet on 13 May, 1887 and at Bath on 11 October, the annual observance of Phillip's birthday. Here I pleaded with the British, 'Don't forget your friends,' enjoining them not to become engulfed with Europe at the expense of all the Old Commonwealth. The press gave this wide reportage, but by then less than two months were to elapse before Britain's admittance to the EEC on New Year's Day 1973. At least it was my final *cri de Coeur.*

We were granted the usual courtesies shown to a retiring High Commissioner. The British Government gave us a charming luncheon in the chandelier room at Marlborough House, presided over by that gracious statesman Alec Douglas-Home. The Agents-General treated us to a splendid evening reception in the Clothworkers' Hall, attending by the Duke of Kent. The Australia House staff exuded generosity with a dinner, presentation of a picture, books, and two silver candlesticks from my personal secretaries. The Queen received us at the Palace, handing us signed framed photographs of herself and Prince Philip. That benefactress of ours, Queen Elizabeth, the Queen Mother, entertained us to luncheon at Clarence House. It was all a little sad, but both of us felt we had served long enough. Hopefully, we set our faces to fresh fields and pastures new.

~ 5 ~

They were somewhat different fields from what I envisaged. For the preceding two years prominent people in England, in politics and commerce, had suggested various openings once I retired from the High Commissionership. In Australia, I realised that with the advent of the Whitlam Labor Government in December 1972, no representational or administrative work would be offered to me from Canberra. But, at the age of sixty-two, I still felt active and made it clear, privately as well as publicly, I was willing to undertake further public service. My primary dedication lay in British-Australian relations: at the close of my term I declared that henceforth my aim was to serve as an unofficial link between Australia and Britain and even other Commonwealth countries as well.

We remained at *Oare* for Christmas with our family – our two youngest were still at school or university respectively – before being officially repatriated in January 1973. This time we flew direct to Los Angeles, joining the P & O *Arcadia* there for Sydney. In Canberra, Gough Whitlam, then understandably exuberant at becoming Prime Minister, along with Margaret his talented wife, gave us a very friendly luncheon at *The Lodge*; others were equally kind including my former Cabinet colleague Paul Hasluck, Governor-General since 1971. Yet immediately we knew that Canberra, whatever our long associations and its pleasant environment, was not for us. Quite simply, there was nothing to do. Placing our home, 10 Mugga Way, on the market presented no problems. Douglas Anthony, the Country Party Leader, purchased it as an investment on behalf of his party organisation. We then set our sights on acquiring a rural property in South Australia, but nothing we were seeking being available, we returned to our family in England in May. In July the University of Birmingham, at the instigation of the Chancellor, Lord Avon, honoured me by making me an honorary Doctor of Laws. The ceremonies occupied two days, including a dinner the night before at which the Chancellor and I spoke, I felt glad my children were present to hear this distinguished statesman, still eloquent, good looking and charming despite years of wretched health. His friendship to us as a family, his interest in Australia form one of the happiest attributes of my later life.

August in Italy, continuing our annual relaxation at Bellagio on incomparable Lake Como; Christmas at Care; then the South Australia again in January 1974 in quest of a new home. This time we succeeded. On 21 April I agreed to buy from Ron Murray *Wirra Wirra*, Mount Crawford, in the Barossa hills. Built at the turn of the century, set amidst a mixture of giant red gums, European and North American trees, with mellowed stone farm buildings presiding over well-tended pastures, we set about planning to transform the house on the Palladian-Georgian style. I was fortunate in finding such a cultivated, sensitive, experienced architect in the person of Reginald Steele. Although, again for family reasons, we spent the remainder of the year in England, it was not wasted time. A constant exchange of plans and ideas with Steele enabled work to begin immediately we entered into possession on 15 January 1975. These plans were fulfilled by excellent Barossa district craftsmen employed by CG Juncken, the contractor selected by our architect. We re-named the estate *Martinsell*, after the high hill over-looking the village of *Oare* in Wiltshire; and thus through 1975 and 1976 came into being what I hope will ever remain as the Downer family base.

Simultaneously, it became inexorably apparent that to maintain a country house the size of *Oare* as well as a country house in Australia, was quite beyond my capacity. Rapid inflation in Britain, ever-rising wages, rates, and service charges reduced places such as *Oare* to resorts of millionaires. Reluctantly, and with sorrow, we placed *Oare* on the market in June 1975. Five months later a rich man bought it in the person of Henry Keswick, well-known in Hong Kong, Scotland and London.

On 14 January 1976 we drove out of *Oare* for the last time, but not before two significant family events.

The first of these was the wedding on the previous 18 October of our eldest girl Stella to Christopher Stevens, a youngish Englishman living in Cognac, France where he is a wine merchant. They chose the neighbouring medieval church of Wilcot for the service, and the recently retired Archbishop of Adelaide, Dr TT Reed to marry them. A luncheon reception for two hundred and fifty guests followed. Some of them, being in the wine trade, made it a lively as well as happy affair.

Our last big party took place on 28 December. Designed primarily to say goodbye to some of our Wiltshire friends, it received an impetus by the attendance of the Governor-General and Lady Kerr. Sir John Kerr, only six weeks before, had caused a sensation throughout the British Commonwealth by dismissing Mr Whitlam and his ministers. Now on a visit to England to report to the Queen, Sir John inevitably became the star turn of our luncheon. I ensured that the guests all met this impressive-looking, controversial figure. On his part, he manifested no inhibitions about discussing those events. Indeed, he told me he could think of little else.

Since that time, I have tried to fulfil my declared intention of acting as some sort of a link between Australia and Britain. None of the suggestions made to me whilst occupying high office in London ever materialised – but this is common disillusionment amongst public men. I am fortunate in my son Alexander, now in the Australian Diplomatic Service. On 17 June 1973 he married Nicola Robinson of Chesterfield, Derbyshire, who will help him in his career. A young man of great promise, he, and equally my three daughters Stella, Angela and Una, have brought me affection, companionship and joy. But life's principal blessing to me is my wife Mary, without whose love, unselfishness and wisdom, half of whatever I have attained would not have been possible.

*Chapter 14*

# Thomas Edward Downer 1913–

Tom Downer provides a contrast with the various lawyers and politicians in the Downer family. His life brings a refreshing breeze of country air which, in part, accounts for his popularity. The only son of Charles, and a grandson of Henry Downer MP, he has spent his life on the land ever since leaving school.

Adelaide was his birthplace on 19 May 1913. His mother, formerly Bertha Law-Smith, belonged to a well known merchant family in South Australia. She was a warm and generous woman, much beloved by her generation. He went to his father's old school, St Peter's, but after nine years during which he did not achieve any outstanding academic distinction, he preferred to gain pastoral experience as a jackeroo rather than to proceed to a university. In 1936 he bought the first of his properties, *Erinka*, south of Woodside, built a pleasant house and improved what were already well-established pastures. Then came the war years: between 1940 and 1945 he served as a gunner in the 2/14 Field Regiment, AIF in Darwin, New Guinea, and Rabaul. The restoration of peace enabled to return to his farming pursuits, as well as to profounder interests. For it was about this time that he fell in love with an Adelaide girl, Monica Jessop: they were married on 8 April 1948, and have found fulfilment not only in one another but in their two sons Charles Michael and James Frank. The next year saw him adding substantially to his acres by the purchase of *Mount Beevor* station in the eastern Mount Lofty Ranges; much later again he acquired *Onaunga* in the same region.

Tom Downer's capacity as a grazier is well-known but he will be remembered more for his expertise as a horseman – a talent inherited from his father, and shared with his uncle

Frank. When only fourteen he rode with the Adelaide Hunt Club; after the War he acted as Master between 1945 and 1948, thereby following in the saddle Frank and his grand-father Henry. Ten years later the Club made him their president, and subsequently their patron. As a polo player he displayed equal skill, playing in the Adelaide team for four seasons preceding World War II. His youthful zest was acknowledged nearly twenty years later by being chosen president of the Adelaide Poo Club from 1968 to 1973.

This interest in horses carried on to his later life. Since 1968 he has been an active Committeeman of the Onkaparinga Racing Club, a useful but mundane task compared with his performance as a driver in one of Australia's most acclaimed films *Picnic at Hanging Rock*. The horses and horse-drawn vehicles in this sensitive, artistic, eerie production where all supplied by Tom Downer.

Throughout his adult life he has shown a fine public spirit. Though eschewing politics – he could never be suspected of radicalism – he has supported charitable causes both financially and by personal action. Into this category comes the South Australian National Trust, in which ever since its establishment he has shown a genuine interest. He is basically a family man, having led an exemplary domestic life loyally supported by his wife. He has certainly shown far more interest in his antecedents, and collateral relations than any of his forebears, as is evidenced by his researchers in South Australia and England.

His sons are continuing the grazing activities of this branch of the family. Charles, the elder, in 1977 married Julie Baverstock of Adelaide and now manages *Erinka*. James, the younger, is similarly occupied at Mount Beevor. Life for Tom Downer has been satisfying despite bouts of indifferent health. He is a praiseworthy example of one who, having inherited considerable wealth, directed it to productive use in further developing parts of his State. Patriotic, possessed of sound judgment, if there were more men like him Australia would have fewer problems.

# Index

## E



## F



## G

## H



## I



## J



## K

## P



## R

## S



## T



## V



## W